CW00370320

Inland Waterways

Charles Hadfield

with text illustrations by
John James

David & Charles
Newton Abbot   London
North Pomfret (Vt)   Vancouver

British Library Cataloguing in Publication Data

Hadfield, Charles
   Inland waterways. – (David & Charles leisure and travel series).
   1. Canals – Great Britain
   I. Title
   386'.46'0941   HE435

   ISBN 0-7153-7502-4

All rights reserved. No part of this
publication may be reproduced, stored
in a retrieval system, or transmitted,
in any form or by any means, electronic,
mechanical, photocopying, recording or
otherwise, without the prior permission
of David & Charles (Publishers) Limited

Typeset by Tradespools Limited, Frome
and printed in Great Britain by
Redwood Burn Limited, Trowbridge & Esher
for David & Charles (Publishers) Limited
Brunel House Newton Abbot Devon

Published in the United States of America
by David & Charles Inc
North Pomfret Vermont 05053 USA

Published in Canada
by Douglas David & Charles Limited
1875 Welch Street North Vancouver BC

Contents

Preface

I hope that this book will prove useful to those who may be attracted by a cruising advertisement or a trip on a hotel boat, but who feel they would like to find out something about canals first. Under the title *Inland Waterways*, and now included in David & Charles's Leisure & Travel Series, it updates an earlier book of mine, *Introducing Inland Waterways*.

The book appears at an interesting time. On the side of cruising, the smaller canals have completed their transition from being the semi-derelict relicts of earlier transport days to being an important part of the nation's holiday and recreational scene. In doing so, they present a problem to those who enjoy, even love, them: to what extent does one try to preserve them as surviving evidences of an earlier transport pattern, complete with examples of eighteenth- and nineteenth-century engineering and architecture? How does one reconcile the present and the past?

Given, too, the successful transition, we see now a tremendous growth of interest in canal restoration, by voluntary bodies, the British Waterways Board, local authorities and, through the job creation scheme, the Government. How motived it is difficult to be sure. Certainly to the practical advantages of increasing the cruising network one must add the enjoyment townsmen – and women – get from hard and preferably dirty manual work in congenial company, together with a measure of the rather sad nostalgia that, perhaps temporarily, runs through life today.

Commercial waterways are also changing. The days of the local canal narrow boat, the small barge even, are gone: the future lies with very big new or modernised waterways, usually rivers, upon which fast-running large craft will ply on long hauls to and from ports, or seagoing ships or barges penetrate inland to riverside wharves. The development of barge-carrying ships also now enables barges to move without transhipment of cargo from this country to the Continent or America. Quite new things are happening at home and abroad to a very old kind of transport.

Every few years, the government of the time proposes to abolish the British Waterways Board, authority for most of Britain's inland waterways, and absorb its functions into those of other bodies. Such a proposal is in White Paper form as I write. Since speculation on what will happen is useless, and the resistance of British people to being messed about increases daily, I have described the waterway scene as it now is.

This book tells the reader something of inland waterways, past and present, at home and abroad. May others find in them the enjoyment they have given me.

Charles Hadfield

Little Venice
October 1977

Acknowledgements

I am most grateful to the following for photographs: Derek Pratt, 1–9, 12, 14, 17–18, 20–2, 24–7; Westminster City Libraries local history collection, 11; British Waterways Board, 13, 15–16, 19; Philip Daniell, 23; Bord Fáilte, 28; Dan Owen, *The Waterways Journal*, St Louis, Missouri, USA, 29; Photo Hugues, 30; William H. Shank, 31; Ministry of Industry & Tourism, Ontario, Canada, 32.

I should also like thankfully to acknowledge the help of the following: Mrs Frances Pratt, Messrs O. H. Grafton and Mr J. W. R. Richardson of the British Waterways Board; Mrs Helen Harris; Mrs Ruth Heard; Major Logan Brown; Capt T. Hahn; Dr Robert Legget; Messrs Mark Baldwin, Geoffrey Brough, Hugh Compton, Brian E. Holden and Ken Parrott. My wife's help, in particular in the section on natural history, in general in enabling me to do what had to be done, was, as always, just what was needed.

1 Come Canalling

If you like quiet and are not in a hurry, many hundreds of miles of waterways through the pastoral heart of England are ready to welcome you. Even in a big town the canal is cut off from the smell and noise of the streets, as any Londoner knows who has cruised between Camden Town and Little Venice on the Regent's Canal. In the country the canal can take you back two hundred years as it winds across the fields miles from a main road, rising gently by trim locks with white-tipped beams. You will see little all day but trees and fields, cottages, boats, and perhaps the flash of a kingfisher or a heron's sudden rise; hear nothing but a tractor or the squawk of a seagull above the hum of your boat's engine. When you stop for lunch, there is the ripple of the bright water and the bushes' reflection to see, and when you go to bed at night, it is to the sound of water over a distant lock-weir, and the scurry of a vole in the bank.

Now and then you will come to a village, where you can shop and spend an hour or two listening to the locals in the pub. Occasionally a small town will offer a wife a meal she has not cooked herself, and all perhaps an evening with the local dramatic society: I enjoyed the Batley Thespians in *The Land of Smiles* all the more for their association with the Calder & Hebble. If you have a map and a guide book, you can leave the canal for an hour or two whenever you like (boats lock up), and set off to find those many 'sights' that lie quite near the water.

Scattered along the waterway you will find people worth meeting. Some will be explorers like yourself, who can advise you on what to see next, whether there is a shallow bit ahead, and where to get sausages. Others will make their living beside or on the water and, if you are interested and in no hurry, they can tell you much worth knowing.

Canalling (I take the word from an eighteenth-century mock-heroic poem) is doing what you like, or doing nothing if you like that better; meeting people and talking, or passing them with a wave; seeing waterside country sights, breathing country air, and absorbing country quiet — unless you like to see how different

'... the water, just that little bit separated from the land.' The Brecknock &
Abergavenny Canal near Goytre

familiar city streets look from the water. Above all, it is being on
the water, just that little bit separated from the land.

If you want to explore the waterways of Britain you need not
have a boat: you can walk along the towpath and put up at villages
on or near the canal – or go by car. Feet, enterprise and a good
town plan are often best for exploring town waterways with all
their intricacies and oddities, but on the whole, it is best to take a
boat. If you do, there are several choices before you.

Hotel Boats

First, there are the hotel boats. These are narrow canal boats which
have been converted into floating hotels. Travellers have nothing
to do but enjoy themselves while they are carried through some of
the best canal scenery in the country.

These craft usually run in pairs, between eight and twelve
passengers being carried on each trip. A typical craft has three
double- and two single-berth cabins with comfortable bunks,
basins with running hot and cold water, and electric light. There is
a large saloon, and a deck where passengers can sit to watch the
world go by. By day you can help to work the locks, or go exploring at the stops; at night the boats moor at some out of the way

'. . . travellers have nothing to do but enjoy themselves.' Hotel boats *Rose of Brecon* and *Abergavenny Castle* on the Llangollen Canal

place where, after a good dinner, you can sleep to country sounds and wake with a better appetite for breakfast than you have had for months.

Hotel boats run to a schedule: you can book for a week or a fortnight, and sometimes for special periods. The cost varies with the time of year. To find out about such boats, see the *Waterway Users' Companion*, or *Waterways World*, or advertisements in the Press.

Camping Boats

Some hiring firms offer these. They may be converted narrow boats accommodating up to twelve people, plus any who like sleeping in a tent, or specially-built pontoons taking four, or something in between. Such boats are either permanently moored, or are semi-motorised, meant to move short distances only.

Sailing

Canals are not suitable for sailing. Yachts can of course be hired on the Broads, the Thames and some other rivers. Canal reservoirs are also used for sailing, but are usually private to a local club. The *Waterway Users' Companion* has addresses of sailing clubs based on canal reservoirs.

Motor Cruisers

Then there are the motor cruisers, the usual form of pleasure transport on waterways. They vary from two to eight or more berths, and usually have gas cooking equipment, a refrigerator, electric light and toilet, and are equipped with all you will need except perhaps for bed linen. Hiring firms will supply this as an extra, or you can bring your own. Diesel or inboard or outboard petrol engines are fitted — on the first time out, there is much to be said for the safety and simplicity of diesel. No driving licence is required — the hirer will give elementary instruction on the boat, the engine and lock working before you start.

Boats can be hired from nearly a hundred hirers based all over the waterways, so you should be able to find one in whatever part of the country you feel like cruising. If, however, you want to use the narrow canals (and except in the north you probably will need to), you must hire a craft narrow enough to pass through the 7 ft wide locks. Such boats can be up to 70 ft long (full narrow boat length), but a novice should perhaps try his hand first on a craft of not more than 45 ft. If you keep to broad canals or rivers, you can of course hire wider craft. Given today's changing prices, it would be useless to quote charges, which in any case vary greatly with the time of year and size of boat. A canal licence is included in the hire charge.

Consult a book like Charles Hadfield's and Michael Streat's *Holiday Cruising on Inland Waterways* for the background to waterway cruising. It tells you what you will want to know about hiring, buying or converting a boat, navigating it, and choosing where to go. The hardback edition includes Stanford's waterways map. Two other books in the same 'Holiday Cruising' series, *Holiday Cruising on the Thames*, by E. & P. W. Ball, and *Holiday Cruising on the Broads and Fens*, by Lewis Edwards, give additional information about these popular cruising grounds. Both have good maps.

Canal cruising has become popular, though few canals could be called crowded. However, there will be people about should you want them, and repair facilities are also available.

To find hirers, write to the Inland Waterways Association, 114 Regent's Park Road, London NW1 8UQ for their annual *Inland*

11

Waterways Guide, which includes a full list. Or look at the advertisements in the monthly *Waterways World*, the boating magazines, or the quality Sunday papers.

Canoes

Canoeing on canals dates back at least to 1867 (the first reference to it that I have), on rivers earlier still. It was made popular by William Bliss, whose books are still worth reading. Canoeists can obtain a licence at a cheap rate, and can of course explore some canals, like parts of the Kennet & Avon, which are closed to craft that cannot be carried round the locks. Canoes can often be hired by the day or week from boat-hiring firms. They are not, however, allowed to pass through tunnels, and therefore you should plan trips away from these.

Trailing

If you trail your own boat, the annual *Getting Afloat* (obtainable from the Inland Waterways Association) is a guide to launching sites. But do not forget that your boat must first be licensed. For British Waterways Board waterways, contact BWB, Willow Grange, Church Road, Watford WD1 3QA (tel: Watford 26422).

'... few canals could be called crowded.' Farnhill near Keighley on the Leeds & Liverpool Canal

'. . . I'm a looker, a leaner on bridge parapets, a sitter on lock beams. . .'. East Farleigh bridge and lock on the river Medway

Day Trips

For most of the year, day-trip boats will be running all over the country, such as those which carry thousands of people each year between Little Venice and the Zoo or Camden Town in London. You will find such trips advertised in canal magazines and locally, and most are also listed in the *Waterways Users' Companion*.

Getting the Feel

To get the feel of inland waterways, I suggest you buy a copy of the monthly *Waterways World*, published by Waterway Productions Ltd, Kottingham House, Dale Street, Burton-on-Trent, Staffs, DE14 3TD. You will find it on most bookstalls. Then turn to Appendix 1 of this book.

Walking and Just Looking

Strictly, most towpaths are not public rights of way, though more and more are being officially opened to the public. On country canals, however, no one will object to you walking as much as you like – so long, of course, as no damage is done and no canal property interfered with. In towns, some paths are open, eg in London from Lisson Grove eastwards by way of the Zoo and later over Islington tunnel to Victoria Park, Hackney, and from near Little Venice westwards to Ladbroke Grove, with extensions planned to Brentford and Uxbridge over paths many of which are already rights of way. For others, you will need a permit. Ask the nearest canal official.

Personally, I'm a looker, a leaner on bridge parapets, a sitter on lock beams, a potterer wherever boats are moored, an investigator of any odd bit of canal or building I find. I just like looking and listening and ferreting about. It's not a bad way to begin canalling.

2 Cruising on Your Own

Most people like to hire a cruiser and find out about the canals for themselves. Many later buy their own boat. Here are a few ideas for the first tripper. Fuller information for those who want to hire, and also those with buying or conversion in mind, will be found in *Holiday Cruising on Inland Waterways*.

Where To Go

The Midland canals and those of Cheshire, Shropshire and Worcestershire are the centre of pleasure boating, especially for the unskilled, though the broad northern canals, some very beautiful and all interesting, are becoming popular.

Especially to be recommended for beauty in the Midlands are:

(a)   the Shropshire Union main line from Chester to Autherley Junction near Wolverhampton, and decidedly the branch from Hurleston to Llangollen, usually called the Llangollen or Welsh Canal;

(b)   the Macclesfield and Peak Forest Canals from Harecastle near Stoke-on-Trent up to Whaley Bridge on the edge of the Peak District;

(c)   the Grand Union from the edge of London to Kingswood not far from the edge of Birmingham;

(d)   the Stratford-upon-Avon Canal from Kingswood to Stratford, and the Avon thence via Evesham to Tewkesbury;

(e)   the Leicester line of the Grand Union from Norton Junction near Daventry via Foxton and Leicester to the Trent;

(f)   the Oxford Canal from Oxford to Hawkesbury near Coventry, and then by a short length of the Coventry Canal to the Ashby-de-la-Zouch Canal.

(g)   the Staffordshire & Worcestershire Canal from Great Haywood, where it joins the Trent & Mersey, to Stourport-on-Severn.

(h)   the Caldon branch of the Trent & Mersey Canal from Etruria, Stoke-on-Trent, to Froghall;

(i)   the Leeds & Liverpool Canal, especially from Bingley to Foulridge near Colne;

Aylesford on the river Medway

(j) the isolated Lancaster Canal from Preston to Tewitfield.

In the South:

(k) the Thames (see *Holiday Cruising on the Thames*), the navigable parts of the Kennet and the Kennet & Avon Canal, the river Wey (controlled by the National Trust), the Stort and Lea.

(l) the river Medway up to Tonbridge.

In the East:

(m) the most popular of all cruising areas, the Broads and their associated rivers;

(n) the Great Ouse and the Fenland waterways accessible from it;

(o) the Nene (access from the canal system at Northampton).

For these last three, see *Holiday Cruising on the Broads and Fens*.

In Scotland:

(p) the Caledonian Canal.

To get the background of cruising, read Frederic Doerflinger's books, *Slow Boat through England* and *Slow Boat through Pennine Waters*, David Owens' *Water Highways*, *Water Rallies* or *Water Byways*, or John Seymour's *Voyage through England*. Don't miss L. T. C. Rolt's *Narrow Boat*, the greatest cruising book of all.

16

Neptune's Staircase, the flight of eight locks on the Caledonian Canal that lead down to Corpach and Loch Linnhe

How Far To Go

If you have not been on the canals before, don't plan too long a cruise in the time you have. Reckon your average speed at 3 mph on narrow canals, and allow 10 minutes for each lock. Then, say 16 miles of canal and 10 locks will give you seven hours of cruising. Add an hour for the odd delay or rain shower, and you'll be moving for eight hours a day – enough if you are to eat comfortably, explore a little, and enjoy a quiet evening glass. Ignoring the Saturday evening when you will take your hired craft away from the yard and get used to it, and the following Saturday morning's short run-in, that will give you 80 miles and 50 locks in a week, or about 200 miles and 120 locks in a fortnight. A greater distance, of course, if there are fewer locks, and *vice versa*. On broad canals and smaller rivers you can raise the calculated speed to 4 mph, but the lock times to $12\frac{1}{2}$ minutes; on big rivers to 5 mph but 15 minutes per lock. On the Broads, where there are no locks, 5 mph. On the other hand, some shallowish canals are slower than 3 mph – allow two on the line to Llangollen.

Suitable trips, circular or there-and-back, can now be worked out from Stanford's *Inland Cruising Map of England* – distances can be calculated from the scale, and locks are marked. This map is also bound into the hardback edition of *Holiday Cruising on Inland Waterways*. This book contains lists of suggested trips, with distances and number of locks. You will also get many ideas from *The Canals Book*.

Once you have chosen some likely routes, find the names of two or three hirers along them, and send for their brochures. From these you should be able to find a boat that suits you. But start your planning early if you want to cruise in the peak periods.

What Month to Choose

Given the English climate, any month between April and October is as likely to give you fine weather as any other, and somehow you don't notice rain so much on a boat! Indeed, April is my own holiday favourite: others swear by May, and I know one man who always chooses the second week of October. If you choose April or May, you have all the beauty of the spring to accompany you along the waterways, but take a high-necked pullover for the evenings, and make sure the boat you hire has some form of heating. October is a lovely month: rain is rare, the banks of the canals are rich in browns and reds; and it is often hot at midday. All you want is a canalside pub for the evenings, and then a gasfire (don't forget some ventilation for it), a game of cards or some good music on the radio.

Roughly, craft are cheapest to hire up to the third week of May or after mid-September; more expensive from mid-May to early July; and most expensive of all from early July to mid-September. But when you share the cost between the number of passengers, and realise that it includes home, transport and amusements, it won't seem too expensive.

Clothes

Take plenty of warm clothing if out of season. There is nothing so depressing as to be cold on holiday. You will need good mackintoshes, rope-soled shoes, walking shoes, and a change of trousers or slacks that may get wet in the grass. There is always much to see, so take a camera and a pair of field glasses.

Encouragement to Novices

The rest of this section contains elementary information about handling boats, other than sailing craft, on canals and rivers. You will find more detailed information in *Holiday Cruising on Inland Waterways*.

The simplest way to learn how to work a lock is to watch someone doing it. If you can't do that, the following notes may help. About half those who hire cruisers on canals have never been either in a cruiser or on a canal before, and what sounds complicated on paper soon sorts itself out on the lockside. In any case, hiring firms will always provide a man to see you through the first lock out from their base.

I have not said anything about engines because most people know something about them, and anyway it doesn't much matter if they don't. They are reliable, and help is never far away if anything should go wrong. I don't understand them myself. The boatyard will explain the simple maintenance routine for your craft before you start.

Lunch-time on Shakespeare's Avon

Nor have I troubled the reader with advice on feeding himself and his crew. If you send your hire firm a list of groceries and other stores a few days before you are due to start, you will find them waiting on the boat. After that, you will be able to shop at villages and towns along the route. Your water tank will have been filled before you start – it can be replenished at lockside taps.

Locks

The terms for the parts of a lock vary in different parts of the country: I give the commonest. A lock enables boats to pass upwards or downwards from one level of canal to another – the rise varies from a few inches to about 12 ft. It usually consists of a pair of bottom gates (those nearest the lower pound or level of the canal) and either one or two top gates, these last resting on a stone, brick or iron sill, the bottom edge of the upper pound. Gates are opened and shut by wooden or iron balance beams. Put your behind against the beam to open the gate, or pull to shut it. Get a firm grip with your feet. Don't get between the beam and the edge of the lock.

Water is let into and out of locks by paddle-gear. The bottom gates will have a paddle (clough, pronounced *clow* in the north) set below water-level on the inside of each gate. These are shutters which, when raised, leave an opening through which water can be run out of the lock, so enabling it to be emptied. The paddle is raised by a paddle-bar which runs vertically up the inside of the gate and protrudes above it. The top has a ratchet which is engaged by a pinion that can be turned by a detachable handle or windlass, and prevented from slipping back by a pawl. You will be lent windlasses by the hiring firm.

The upper gates may not have paddles set into the gates themselves, but only in the ground beside them. These paddleposts control ground paddles in culverts that pass through the sides of the lock and admit water from the upper pound. Some locks have both ground and gate paddles.

Old paddles can be heavyish, though the new pattern being fitted by the British Waterways Board is a two-finger job. Draw (wind up) paddles slowly, and make sure the pawl clicks round as you do so; if it does not, the windlass will fly round as soon as you take your weight off it. When you drop (lower) a paddle, release the pawl while taking the weight on the windlass, and then wind it steadily down. Do not release it with a bang (some do this with the unlikely idea that they will be mistaken for professionals), or let go of the windlass while it is on a paddle. If the paddle-bar is sticking up above the gate, it is open; if it is down, the paddle is shut.

If you are a crew of two, you will both have to land, one being in charge of the lines to the boat while the other works the lock. If you have three, one can stay on board, and you can motor in and out. If you have a spare also, you can send him on ahead to get the next lock ready.

Types of lock

Locks may be (a) narrow, usually with only one top gate; (b) broad, with two top gates; (c) built as a staircase, the top gate of one lock being the bottom gate of the next above.

Ascending a narrow lock

If it is empty, both get ashore below the lock and tow the boat in, stopping half way up the chamber. If you go too near the front, you may get swamped by the gate paddles; if too near the back, the boat may get hit by the closing gates.

If the lock is full, you must empty it first. One holds the boat by both bow and stern lines, well away from the lock gates – at least 60 ft – because of the undertow as the lock empties. The other shuts the top gates if they are open, then drops the top ground and gate paddles, draws the bottom gate paddles, and waits for the lock to empty, watching to see the boat is not being pulled towards the gates by the undertow. If you lean your behind against the lock beam, you will feel the gate begin to move when the water levels have equalised, and can then push it open. Then walk down to take one of the boat's lines, and together tow the boat in.

One then holds it, again with both lines, while the other shuts the gate and drops the lower paddles. Then he walks to the upper gate to open the ground paddles. If there are gate paddles also, don't use them until the lock is partly full and the worst of the turbulence is over, or you will throw the boat about in the lock.

If, however, you have a biggish boat, eg a cut-down narrow boat, then you need not use lines. Motor in, take her right up until the bow gently touches the top sill. Keep her there in forward gear, with the engine running slowly. If you do this, your crew member working the lock must not use the gate paddles until the lock is about half full, or he will put water into the boat. Whoever works the lock must watch the boat during the whole process, to see no water splashes in, that there is not too much turbulence due to the water being admitted too quickly, and that the boat has not got caught on anything. If anything does go wrong, drop all paddles as quickly as possible. Then sort it out.

When the water level inside the lock reaches that outside, open the top gate to let the boat out. Do not push it open with the boat – it's bad for both. Before you leave, see all paddles are closed (paddle-bars down), and as you leave the lock, close the top gate after you.

Ascending a broad lock

As before. If you have a narrow-beam boat, you need only open and shut one gate. Always use lines to hold her in a broad lock.

Draw the ground paddle on the same side of the lock as the boat first; this tends to hold the boat against the wall. Then the gate paddle on the opposite side to the boat; then the ground paddle on that side. Don't use the gate paddle on the boat side at all. Open all paddles slowly and carefully, watching the boat as you do so. Too much turbulence can cause the boat to swerve about in the chamber and make it difficult to hold her. If you are nervous, take a turn with the line round a bollard or lock beam.

Ascending a staircase pair of locks

To start with, you want the upper lock full and the lower one empty. So go to the top gates and make sure the paddles are dropped. Then empty the lower lock and enter. Close the gates, drop the paddles, and draw those on the centre gates. Water will then pass from the upper to the lower lock. It is not easy to judge when it is quite full, and you may find that you must restrain yourself from trying to open the centre gates too soon. Open the centre gates and pass into the upper lock. Close them, drop their paddles, and proceed to fill the upper lock as for an ordinary lock.

Alongside multi-lock staircases you will find a notice board with full instructions.

Ascending a flight of locks

If you have a spare crew member, send him on to make ready the lock next ahead, unless a boat is coming the other way.

The flight may have side-ponds to the locks. If so, you will find a

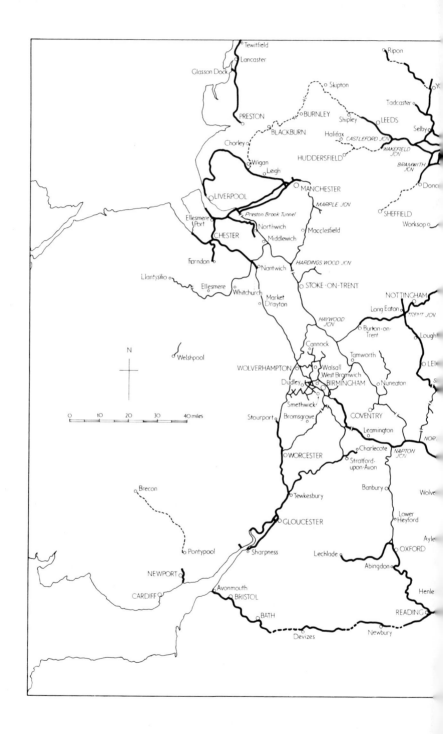

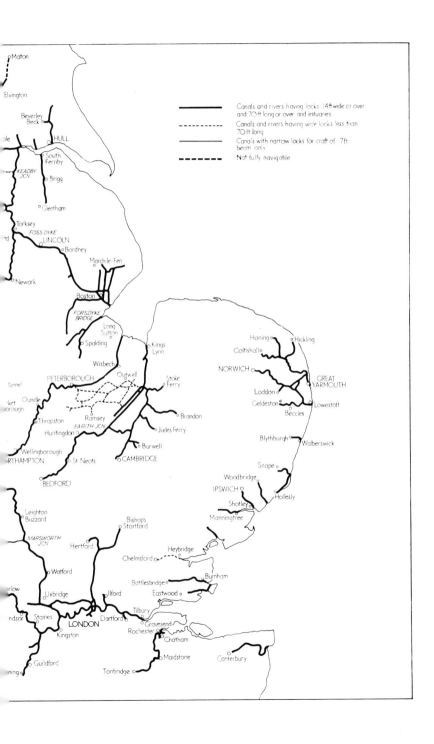

Canals and rivers having locks 14ft wide or over
and 70ft long or over and estuaries

Canals and rivers having wide locks less than
70ft long

Canals with narrow locks for craft of 7ft
beam only

Not fully navigable

board with instructions on what to do, or the lock-keeper will help you. Side-ponds are there to save water. The principle is that on going up you draw roughly half a lockful from each side-pond and half from the lock above; coming down, you put about half a lockful into each side-pond, and half into the lock below. Therefore a boat going either way uses about half a lockful altogether instead of a whole lockful. To save water when possible is everyone's job, not just the other person's.

Descending a narrow lock

If it is ready for you, ie full, open the gate, enter, and shut the gate, dropping the top gate paddles if they are open. If it is against you, ie empty, let one member of your crew hold the boat on two lines, bow and stern, against the towpath well back from the lock gates. Then shut the bottom gates and drop their paddles, open the top ground and gate paddles to fill the lock, open the top gate, tow the boat in, and shut the gate and drop the top gate and ground paddles.

The boat should be held towards the far end of the lock, with her stern well away from the top gate sill. Watch this especially if you are sharing the lock with another boat.

Draw the bottom gate paddles to let the water out of the lock, watching the boat to see she does not drift back on to the sill. When the lock is empty, open the bottom gates and take the boat out, dropping the paddles on the way. If the top gate leaks badly, close the bottom gates also.

Descending a broad lock

As above. In canal locks, it is usually best to hold the lines from the lockside, letting them out as the boat falls in the lock. But on big river locks like those on the Thames, where you do not work the lock yourself, the usual practice is to take a line, fastened to a centre cleat on the boat, round a lockside bollard, then back on board. Hold the end, don't fasten it, because as the boat falls, you will need to let it out. When you are ready to leave the lock, drop the end you are holding, and pull the line in from the fixed end.

General points about locks

Share a lock with another boat if possible. It saves water and work.

If you see another boat approaching a lock that is ready for it, let it go through first.

Don't feel everything has to be done at top speed. If a high-efficiency crew comes up behind you, let them through first, then take your time. That's what canalling is really about. As you motor away from a lock, get into the habit of looking back to see all paddle-bars are right down. If one is a little open, water can run through the lock until the pound empties. Swallow your annoyance and go back.

If the lock is an old one, go especially carefully, and keep clear of the water that will pour through the top gates when you empty the lock. If the gates won't open properly, look behind them for bits of timber or floating cans. Clear these out: don't try to squeeze past, or you may jam the boat in the gate opening.

Care of Water

The present popularity of canal cruising puts a strain on canal water supplies in most years. The more everybody takes trouble to save water, the more there will be for others later in the season – or even next season. Therefore where possible share a lock with another boat, even if it means waiting a few minutes. If you are one of two boats approaching a lock from opposite directions, the one to take it is the one for whom it is ready ie if it is full, the upper boat; if empty, the lower one. At a staircase, have patience: as long as the movement of boats is one way, each passage of the flight only uses one lockful of water, but as soon as the direction changes, the water taken from the upper pound equals the total of all the lock chambers in the staircase. Finally, if side ponds are provided at locks, use them in spite of the small extra trouble.

Moving Along a Canal

You can take it that the canal bottom slopes gradually to its greatest depth in the middle, and that the water gets shallower towards the edges. Therefore keep to the middle. On curves the deep channel will run on the outside of the curve, and there will be a mudbank on the inside. So don't try to cut the corners.

When meeting a boat, keep to the right. You can both keep near the centre – three feet between the boats when passing is enough.

Slow down when passing moored boats. If you don't, you can

upset a kettle that someone is boiling on the moored craft's gas stove, or even tear the boat from its moorings. Slow also for fishing matches or regattas.

Respect fishermen in canals and rivers: they enjoy fishing as you enjoy boating, and each of you has paid to do it. Keep away from their lines, and remember that you and they are each nuisances to the other.

When you cannot see right round a curve in front, or where there is a bridge-hole with a curve beyond it, slow down, sound your horn, and listen for an answer. If you get one, stop, and wait for him to appear. If he doesn't, proceed dead slow. If you hear a horn, reply to it, and proceed slowly. Never see if you have time to get through – he may be bigger than you.

The speed limit is usually 4 mph on canals (6 mph on rivers), but there are exceptions, which your hirer will tell you. The Welsh (Llangollen) Canal with its 2 mph limit is one of them.

Whatever the limit, don't travel so fast that you create a breaking wave. It erodes the banks and can inconvenience or endanger moored craft, anglers and wild life. If you create a breaking wave on one side of the canal but not on the other, you are out of the channel. Move away from the wave. You'll come across the occasional water-hog or canal cowboy. Do what you can politely to teach him better ways. If politeness gets you nowhere, report his boat to the first canal official you see or can contact.

If you run aground, go astern. Don't use your engine, however, if there's any grinding sound astern which indicates that your propeller is hitting stones. Get your crew right aft to raise the bow, and then use the shaft to push off backwards. If she is sluggish, rock her to get her loose, and then use the shaft. At the worst, throw a line to someone on the bank, and get him to pull.

Slow down for a bridge-hole. Just under the bridge may be shallow with rubbish thrown from the bridge. I coast through in neutral – this brings the stern up, and so I am less likely to pick up something on the propeller. If I do, it will be easier to get it off.

If you do pick something up while the propeller is at work, try going astern and then ahead to throw it off. If you can't, pull into the bank and get at it through the weed hatch, or poke at it with the shaft. If you still can't clear it, you may have to strip and get

Two well-behaved cruisers on the river Wey near Godalming. Neither is creating a breaking wave or incommoding the moored cruiser – and the swans

down to it. I hope you won't. I've only once had real trouble – with a long length of electric flex. It cost me a breadknife to get it off.

Don't attempt to navigate at night until you are experienced. In any case, your terms of hire may prohibit it.

Mooring

On most canals there are recognised mooring lengths, signposted, and with rings provided.

If not at moorings, choose a place a little way above or below (but not at) a lock or bridge-hole, well out of the way of passing boats, and not on a bend. Failing that, choose a place on the towpath side where you can get in close to the edge. Bring your bow gently into the bank so that one of your crew can jump ashore holding a rope attached to the centre of your boat; go into neutral as soon as he is ashore, and let him pull the boat gently into the bank. Once alongside, use bow and stern lines to spikes driven into the ground between the towpath and the water. Don't have lines across the towpath: someone may get hurt. Before mooring, check that your propeller is clear of underwater stones, otherwise the wash of passing boats may cause it to hit them.

When leaving your mooring, start your engine and put it in neutral, get your lines in, and push the stern off first from the bank with your shaft without using the engine. When the stern is well out from the bank, put her in reverse and back out into the centre of the canal. Then straighten up and go forward. In this way you will not damage your propeller.

Remember that the side of the canal away from the towpath is private property.

Turning

When turning round (called winding on canals, with the 'i' short, as in 'windy'), do not use the engine unless there is plenty of room, for fear of damaging the propeller. Choose a place where the canal is wide, take a stern rope and shaft on to the towpath, put the bow into the opposite bank, and pull her round with the rope, holding the rudder off with the shaft. Along the canals you will come across widened parts, where the narrow boats used to turn. You can of course use these, having checked that there is enough depth:

some have been dredged, some haven't.

If you want to turn in a walled basin or similar spot with plenty of water, put your bow gently into the wall and your helm over in the direction you want to turn, and have your engine slow ahead. She will come gently round. At the last minute go astern and back out before going ahead in the opposite direction.

Swing or Drawbridges

Swing bridges pivot, and are moved by a handle that you push, or by a windlass. Drawbridges lift. Some are counterbalanced, like those on the Oxford Canal, and a grown-up – not a youngster – holds down one end and so raises the bridge. Others have an overhead framework: by pulling down one end of it, the other end pulls up a section of roadway. Many of these have a hanging chain with which to pull down the top bar: if it is not there, hook your shaft over the bar to draw it down.

If there are safety gates, put these in position across both road approaches before opening the bridge. If no gates are provided detail a member of your crew to watch for traffic and warn it.

Close all bridges after you.

Tunnels

Some were built for 7 ft wide narrow boats only. When you get to such a tunnel, if it is short, look to see if a boat is approaching before you enter: if it is, you will see its light. In that case, wait. The long narrow tunnel at Harecastle near Stoke-on-Trent is normally controlled by tunnel-keepers at each end, to whom you should report before entering; at weekends or bank holidays on a time basis that is set out on notice-boards at the entrances. (At present, boats go north from dawn to 11 am, south from 1 pm to dusk. The time-gap is to allow all boats which have already entered the tunnel to clear it.) In broad tunnels, two narrow cruisers can pass easily enough. Drop to slow to pass, but not so slow that you lose steerage way, and keep to the right.

Tunnels are nothing to be alarmed about. Switch on your headlight, and take them slowly. Give a long blast on your horn before you enter, in case a boat's light has failed, and also before you come out again. For longer tunnels, put on a mackintosh –

'Tunnels are nothing to be alarmed about.' A cruiser leaves Ellesmere narrow-boat tunnel on the Llangollen Canal

you can get quite wet from water coming down the ventilation shafts. Before you enter, put young children in the cabin, and have others under supervision – it's disturbing to come out of a tunnel with fewer children than when you went in.

Canoes are not allowed in tunnels.

If you have a nervous crew member, she (or he) can walk over the top, using the old path the towing horses took.

Lock-keepers

Only on the Thames, and on commercial waterways like the Aire & Calder, Severn and Trent, are the lock-keepers there to work the locks. On most canals they are widely scattered, and may not be at the locks at all. If they are, their job is not to work the locks for you, but to see that you do it properly, do not waste water, and leave them in good order. Should a lock-keeper help you by getting a number of locks ready for you (ie filling or emptying them ready for you to enter), it would be tactful to offer a tip. Not all will accept it.

Treat lock-keepers with courtesy. It will usually be returned. If it is not, remember that not all holiday-makers are as sensible as you are, and the lock-keeper may have struck some of the others recently. Most such men are well worth talking to, mines of information about the canals and their surroundings.

Maps and Guides

I never go anywhere without the 1:50,000 Ordnance Survey maps for the country I propose to pass through. One can miss a great deal without them.

For waterways controlled by the British Waterways Board, you will find *Nicholson's Guides to the Waterways* full of useful information as well as providing a canal map based on the $2\frac{1}{2}$ OS. There are four volumes: South East, North West, South West, North East: respectively they cover 440, 530, 371 and 343 miles of waterway. The Ladyline Cruising Guides are a series based on individual canals. There are also some other guides to particular waterways – all are listed by the Inland Waterways Association in their saleslist. You will also find much information in the IWA's *Inland Waterways Guide*.

Unless you are already a naturalist, I suggest you take a bird and a flower book with you. For the first two or three days you will be too interested in handling the boat and working locks to stop and look – but later you may.

In General

If all the people who participate in canal life are to enjoy themselves, then follow the rules you would like them also to follow: don't speed, don't make unnecessary noise, don't leave litter, respect wild life. Don't be in too much of a hurry. Help those who are less experienced than you, and don't be afraid to ask what you yourself would like to know.

I hope you have many happy days of canalling.

3 How We Got Our Canals

Early Days

The Fossdyke from Torksey on the Trent was built by the Romans, for navigation as well as drainage. Except for this, the Exeter Canal was Britain's first commercial canal. It was built in the reign of Elizabeth I from Countess Wear to Exeter to by-pass obstructions in the river. By 1566, however, when it was opened, the principal rivers of England were carrying a good deal of traffic, some of it coal.

Barges using rivers still in their natural state were much hindered by shallows, rapids and periods of flood, for they needed enough water to float them over shallows, and enough man or horse power to drag their heavy bulk against current and even floodwater. In those days there were also many riverside mills, using water-power not only to grind corn, but for all industrial processes that needed power, and at each mill a weir crossed the river to impound the water required to drive the mill-wheel. Barges could pass through a movable section of this weir, called a flash-lock, but they had to wait until the miller could spare the water he would lose by opening the weir – or the bargemen had to pay him to do so. When the movable section was lifted, water ran over the sill until the level of river below was nearly equal to that above. Then the barge was winched up through the gap or allowed to run downwards.

Except for the weirs, the lower lengths of big rivers were more or less navigable. Pressure for improvement came mainly to the smaller streams and tributaries, upon which pound-locks (those we call locks today) were built to reduce the speed of the current and increase depth over the shallows. Though such rivers as the Lea and the Warwickshire Avon had by then been made navigable, improvements mostly date from after the Civil War, even more from early years of the eighteenth century. Many rivers, among them the Medway, Wey, Kennet, Bristol Avon, Weaver and Aire & Calder had by then been made navigable, and about 1,200 miles were passable for barges carrying coal and other cargoes which otherwise could only have been taken by packhorse or heavy waggon over the roads of the time.

The Industrial Revolution

By the middle of the eighteenth century the Industrial Revolution was under way. The inventors were doing their part, but the potential leap-forward was waiting for better means of transport to enable bricks, slates and timber for building, raw materials to supply factories, food and coal to feed and warm their inhabitants, to be brought to the new industrial towns, and the products of their machines to be carried away. Soon coal for power-raising was demanded, as works went over from water to steam. This period was also the threshold of the Agricultural Revolution, which demanded great quantities of limestone to be burnt into lime for land improvement, materials for new farm buildings and stone for country roads. Transport better than pack-horses and parish roads was needed for all these, and also for carrying away the increased produce of the land. Three such means were found: canals especially for coal, iron, building materials, heavy merchandise, stone, timber, salt, limestone, corn, and imported groceries in bulk; horse-operated tramroads using small 2-ton waggons on iron rails, mainly from collieries and works to canals; and turnpike roads for passengers and goods valuable in proportion to their weight.

This transport system, heavily aided by coastal ships which themselves moved well inland up rivers and into canals, served Britain for nearly a century. Canals, horse tramroads and turnpike roads were extensively built during this time. To some extent, too, the turnpikes began to carry heavier goods as their engineering improved; on the other hand, some waterways went into the business of running fast boats (called fly-boats) for parcels and high-toll consignments, and of carrying passengers in packet-boats on regular services and excursions. Broadly, however, waterways and tramroads remained carriers of heavy and bulk cargoes, while turnpikes carried passengers and light goods.

By 1840 there were in Great Britain about 4,000 miles of inland waterways, some 2,500 miles of horse tramroad, and 22,000 miles of turnpikes. By their means the Industrial Revolution flourished, and the Agricultural Revolution enabled a population which had doubled since 1760 to be fed. Thenceforward the addition of steam railways and ships to the list made it possible for Britain to make greater use of the resources that earlier transport methods had so largely created.

Narrow and Wider

The barges used on the early river navigations were of many sizes, according to the depth and width of the rivers and the traffic to be carried, from 20 or 30 tonners up to the biggest Thames and Kennet barges of some 135 tons.

The first two industrial canals, the Sankey Brook (later called the St Helens) and the Bridgewater, were each built with broad locks (usually 14 ft 6 in or more) to take craft carrying some 60 tons. But the Bridgewater Canal was directly connected to the Duke of Bridgewater's coalmines at Worsley, the workings of which were served by much narrower canals.* These used small boats 47 ft long and $4\frac{1}{2}$ ft wide, into which coal was loaded in containers. The boats were then towed in trains to Manchester for their containers to be off-loaded. These mine boats were almost certainly the forerunners of the later narrow boat.

James Brindley was resident engineer of the Bridgewater Canal, and it was he who prepared plans for the next important canal, the Trent & Mersey or Grand Trunk, which was to take Bridgewater barges at one end and Trent river barges at the other, but narrow boats about 72 ft by 7 ft in the section from Burton-on-Trent to Middlewich in between. His reasons were cheapness of construction, especially in building locks and cutting the $1\frac{5}{8}$ mile long Harecastle tunnel near the Potteries, and economy of water use (a narrow lock uses about 28,000 gallons a time, a barge lock 60,000). Capital was scarce, and in those early days of the Industrial Revolution around the 1760s and 1770s, heavy traffic was not envisaged.

Once the Trent & Mersey's dimensions had been settled, those canals planned to connect with it, all of them having Brindley as their consulting engineer, were built the same size – the Staffs & Worcs to the Severn, the Birmingham, the Coventry and its continuation to the river Thames, the Oxford Canal. So in turn were their branches. A band of narrow canals taking boats capable of carrying up to 30 tons spread across central England.

Other canal engineers and canal managements did not agree

The old days: a narrow boat under Chester's city walls

with Brindley. Notable among dissenting engineers were John Longbotham and John Smeaton, between them responsible for getting started the two earliest important broad canals, the Leeds & Liverpool over the Pennines and the Forth & Clyde across Scotland's waist. They were followed by William Jessop and John Rennie. Rennie built the Lancaster and the Kennet & Avon, both broad, and Jessop a large number of river navigations and broad canals, notably the Rochdale, also over the Pennines, the Trent Navigation and many of the waterways linking with it, and the Grand Junction from the Midlands to London. Just as Brindley only built two larger canals, the Bridgewater and the Droitwich, so Jessop only built one narrow one, the Ellesmere (part is now the Llangollen Canal) and that only because the plans were changed.

* For these mine canals, see C. Hadfield and G. Biddle, *The Canals of North West England*, Chapter 1.

The old days: puzzle picture involving a steamer, coal barges and a towing horse at Warwick Avenue bridge, Little Venice. Whatever is happening interests the spectators

The arguments in favour of larger craft were seen at the time. Jessop, for instance, said that narrow boats would prove uneconomic. Companies and carrying firms involved at points of junction between broad and narrow quickly appreciated the disadvantages of two boat sizes, coping as they did with the same break of gauge problems that later beset railways. Indeed, we can perhaps see Brindley and Brunel as the odd men out, and equate Smeaton with George Stephenson and Jessop, his pupil, with Robert Stephenson.

Handicaps and Efforts

When railway competition began, the narrow canals fatally handicapped waterway competition, especially because many of them ran through key industrial areas, notably Birmingham. Physically, they could not be enlarged because building had closed in on them. So long-distance traffic left them, and only a declining local trade was left. The broad canals lasted longer and fared better, the still larger river navigations best of all, for their locks could more easily be widened and their beds deepened.

As on the Continent, many British waterways could have been adapted, enlarged and modernised to complement the new railway system and later the new road system built after the introduction of the motor lorry, if the State had chosen to do it, as continental governments did choose. This could have been done in spite of the narrow canals, which had no equivalent across the Channel. But we did not choose. Modernisation was therefore sporadic, and mostly limited to a few rivers: notably the Aire & Calder, the Weaver and the Severn in the nineteenth century, the Trent in the early part of the twentieth, followed by a part of the Grand Union Canal in the thirties (the only major canal rebuilding this century) and the Aire & Calder again in our own times.

One great new line of canal was, however, built and opened in 1894 – the Manchester Ship Canal, financed by both private and public money. Its construction led to a revival of interest in large waterways, and a number of new or enlarged canals, eg to Birmingham, were seriously discussed. One indeed, the Sheffield & South Yorkshire, to enlarge the route to Doncaster, Rotherham and Sheffield, was begun, but failed to get away from railway influence.

Royal Commission to Transport Commission

At the turn of the century, interest revived again and led to the appointment of a Royal Commission in 1906. It reported in 1909 in favour of setting up a government Waterways Board, which would rebuild to a larger size the canals in the Cross – that is, those connecting the Mersey, Severn, Thames and Humber with their main traffic feeders – though the Commission could not find a solution to the problem of the narrow Birmingham canals at the centre of the Cross, which could not be economically widened. More attention might have been given to the Commission's recommendations had it not been for the many excitements of the time – the Parliament Act, suffragettes, the Ulster question, and the approach of World War I.

The time between the wars saw a steady decline in the tonnage carried and the closing of a number of waterways, though it also saw the building of modern locks on the Trent, the creation of the Grand Union Canal Company from ten smaller concerns, and the substantial improvements of the waterway to Birmingham. In World War II the canals played their part, helped by women recruited as additional crews, but on balance the canals lost both boatmen and traffic.

By 1945 the tonnage carried had fallen from about 30 millions at the beginning of the century to about 10 millions. From the turn of the century the waterways had been subjected to motor lorry competition, as before they had struggled against railways, and much of this fall in tonnage must be attributed to this cause.

The Transport Act of 1947 brought most of the remaining waterways, those still independent, those already State-owned, and those previously under railway control, under the Docks & Inland Waterways Executive of the British Transport Commission. Some waterways were not, however, nationalised, notably the Manchester Ship Canal and the Bridgewater Canal belonging to it, the Thames, the Yorkshire Ouse, the whole system of navigable rivers that is based on the Great Ouse and the Nene, and the inland waterways of East Anglia.

Towards the Future

The Transport Commission took the first steps towards a future for waterways rather than away from a past. For this much credit goes to Sir Reginald Kerr, who was in charge of them. Now, for the first time, the miscellany of canals Britain possessed began to be separated out according to their likely futures. A good deal of money was spent to begin modernising the biggest, while pleasure cruising was encouraged on the smaller ones. The first hire-craft business on a canal had been founded by G. F. Wain and others near Chester in 1935: as Inland Hire Cruisers Ltd it still flourishes. After the war they were followed by the Wyatts at Stone, Capt L. Munk of 'Maidboats', Michael Streat at Braunston, and others, including the Commission itself with its own boats.

When in 1962 the Commission was broken up, the newly established British Waterways Board carried the division farther. Deciding that the future of the smaller canals was in pleasure boating, the Board planned the cruiseway system that was given permanence in the Transport Act of 1968, and also initiated a highly successful policy of co-operation with volunteers from canal societies to restore lengths of canal that could later be added to the system. By the 1968 Act, also, local authorities were empowered to grant money towards amenity canal development. The cruiseway network, co-operation with volunteers, and the injection of additional local money, has led to a quick growth of the pleasure mileage.

On the transport side the Board set up what became Freight Services Division, responsible for their fleets of boats, warehouses and small docks. Though handicapped by lack of Government interest in inland water transport, it yet managed to transform its image from an old-fashioned to a very modern one.

Then, at the end of 1971, the Government announced that the Board in its turn would be abolished in 1974, its functions being taken over by a number of Regional Water Authorities responsible for all aspects of water supply and use, only to change its mind a year later and retain the Board. Other navigations formerly under River Authorities, however, passed to the new Water Authorities, while others were unaffected. It is safe to say that pleasure traffic on the canals will continue to grow quickly as more people discover their attractions. For water transport also the prospect may be changing for the better.

In July 1977 the Government issued a White Paper, 'The Water Industry in England and Wales: the Next Steps', which proposed the absorption of the British Waterways Board by a National Water Authority, with the possibility of then setting up a National Navigation Authority. Freight transport by waterway was almost completely ignored.

4 Canals at Work

British waterways used for freight carrying are in a transitional state.

In the past they played three roles. First and most important, they were raw material and finished goods carriers between points of origin and use, eg they carried coal from a waterside colliery to a factory sited alongside the water in order to receive it easily, or to a town wharf whence it was distributed to consumers. Second, they were long and medium distance carriers of all kinds of merchandise as part of the country's general transport system. In both roles they were helped by many horse tramroads built to bring them traffic from more distant mines and works, and by side roads from turnpikes. Steam railway competition began by biting heavily into merchandise carrying by water until little was left. It also tended to take over all transport between newly-opened mines and works, leaving canals only the older ones, destined in time to be worked out. This meant the decline and extinction of the horsedrawn tramroads, while cargoes off the side-roads fell away as rail took over much traffic formerly carried on turnpikes. There was, however, some compensation in the building of canal-rail inter-change points, notably in the Birmingham area.

Their third role, however, was as part of the country's coastal and foreign shipping facilities. For instance, craft ran from Leeds by the Aire & Calder to Goole or Hull, and then transhipped their cargoes directly overside to ships. Sometimes there was no transhipment, the craft itself running right through to London, another coastal port, or even to the Continent.

The original threefold pattern was indeed fractured more by the growth of the motor lorry than by railways, for the lorry added to its ability to pick up and discharge door-to-door loads an increasing capacity for long-distance transport as trunk roads improved and motorways were introduced. The first two roles of the waterways have died away to shadows of their former selves; the third remains, and on its foundations it is likely that future development will be built.

For historical, national and political reasons Britain and continental countries have over the last three-quarters of a century taken rather different attitudes to transport. On the Continent, people are more accustomed to thinking of transport as a whole, within which waterway, road, rail, shipping and pipeline carriers each do what they can do best, the State trying to hold the ring so that the best total result is obtained. It is not, of course, as tidy as that, but all the same, the idea of transport integration is there and is influential with governments who have the money for large-scale development.

In Britain, however, we are much less accustomed to think of transport as a whole; much more liable to think of roads, railways, waterways and the rest as each separate, each competing against the rest, as if in theory each could do everything. Moreover, whereas in turnpike days roads had to 'pay', no one has expected them to do so for a century. It would probably not occur to anyone that roads should earn interest on the capital cost of their original construction and of every subsequent reconstruction: yet, until recently, that is what railways and waterways were expected to do. Indeed, railways and waterways are still expected to 'pay', not in terms of total benefit to the community, but in those of hard cash. And not only as a whole. Each proposed new or reconstructed waterway and railway has to be shown as able to 'pay' by itself; yet no-one even thinks of suggesting that a single section of new road should not be built unless it can be shown in advance to 'pay' – that is, to cover maintenance expenses, plus interest on and amortisation of capital.

What, then, of waterways as we approach the 1980s? If we can judge by experience on the Continent, they still have a part to play in our own transport system. But they can best play it if certain conditions apply:–

(a) they are at their best on long hauls, where their economy of man and engine power in relation to tonnage carried can show itself. The average continental haul is about 200 miles; owing to the absence of national waterway statistics, ours is not known, but is probably around 40 miles, with the longest haul in late 1977 being 90 miles. Therefore any increase of haul will improve efficiency;

(b) they are best used by big craft: by ships, or large self-

The *River Avoca* passes one of the mechanised Saltersford locks on the river Weaver in Cheshire

propelled barges moving singly (or one pushing another, a common continental practice), or a push-tug pushing a train of lighters in front of it. Hence waterways must be big and deep, they must have plenty of water (this can be pumped back round the locks and re-used), and craft must be able to move fast and if necessary round the clock. This requires good waterway track: banks piled, bends eased, well-dredged, lit for night travel, with a few large fully mechanised locks rather than many small hand-worked ones, the barges fitted with, eg two-way radio and other naviga-tion aids. All this, equivalent to the apparatus behind modern railways and roads, is common enough on the Continent;

(c) they are best used when craft can load directly from producer and at the other end unload direct to consumer or ship, eg from refinery to tank farm, from colliery to power station, from ore-carrying ship to user works, from waterside factory to ship or distribution warehouse. Therefore if water trans-port is to be properly used, industry that can benefit from water carriage must be invited to settle on waterside to eliminate transhipment, as, for instance, has been so successfully done at Ghent in Belgium;

(d) waterways are best used in co-operation with, and not in competition with, other forms of transport. For instance, if we want to reduce heavy road transport through big cities to docks, we should build transhipment points inland from, eg London, so that traffic brought down the motorways can then be transferred to water to be taken through London by lighter on the Thames and the Lea. The further inland the transhipment takes place, and the longer the waterway haul, the better economically and environmentally – and modern canals built as extensions to the existing river navigations can do this. The British Waterways Board already runs such a transhipment service on a small and very successful scale, with its export barge groupage services from Brentford and Enfield;

(e) moreover, an invention of the last twenty years, the barge-carrying ship, is already in operation in two different forms: Seabee 844 ton capacity lighters, and LASH, 370 tons, working between the United States, Britain at Gravesend or Sheerness on the Thames, and continental ports. The barge-carrying ship greatly alters the old picture, for it both enables the haul by water to be considerably extended and provides a service of containers larger than those which can possibly be carried by road or rail. LASH lighters can, and do, now travel without transhipment from ports well up the Mississippi and its tributaries to others on the Rhine right up to Basle. Lighters are lifted on to the barge-carrying ship by her own crane or lift in an estuary, and without the ship having to dock; and at the end of the voyage lowered back into the water to continue their journey in front of a push-tug.

Allied to the barge-carrying ship concept, are those of the seagoing barge and linked tug-barge. They too must be taken into account in future planning.

Waterways are now in transition. In Britain they still keep, and could develop, an inland transport role, especially if hauls are lengthened and modern water roads, equivalent to motorways, are built. But their future probably lies more with overseas trade, especially through the North Sea and Channel ports; goods loaded at factories built alongside modern waterways, or at road/canal transhipment points, will be taken by water for loading overside at docks or for carriage by barge-carrying ship or seagoing barge to the Continent and the United States. It lies also in encouraging coasting and short sea trade ships to come further inland, by deepening channels, raising bridges, etc.

More than oddly, the Government issues no national inland waterway track and freight statistics comparable with those available for roads and railways. Taking inland waterways as being upstream of the outer limits of ports, the annual tonnage carried is some 60 millions, even though very little government money is given to freight waterway improvement and enlargement.

The future for waterways straddles inland and overseas transport. Other means do also: road transport uses roll-on roll-off ships, railways use rail ferries and press for a Channel Tunnel. But waterways have the sea, which is free, is all round our coasts, and joins our waterways to those of other countries, and especially the Continent.

In the light of what has been written above, what can be seen by the interested?

The narrow-boat, that tough survivor from the eighteenth century, has almost disappeared except as a pleasure boat hull, whether a conversion or a newly-built job. At the time of writing, working narrow-boats can be seen between Brentford and Boxmoor on the Grand Union main line or, more regularly, in combination with northern short-boats in the area of Thurmaston lock on the Leicester section of the Grand Union. Eily Gayford well describes what life on war-time working boats was like in *The Amateur Boatwomen*.

The 60–100 ton barge, more economic, still survives and can be found working: in late 1977, for instance, in the Doncaster area of the Sheffield & South Yorkshire Navigation; between Calder Grove, near Wakefield, and Dewsbury on the Calder & Hebble; on the river Hull and Beverley Beck between Hull and Beverley; and on the Yorkshire Ouse up to York.

Bigger barges and tankers of 100 up to 600 tons and more can be seen on the Aire & Calder between Goole and Leeds, the Trent downstream of Nottingham, the Gloucester & Sharpness ship canal between Sharpness and Gloucester, the Severn up to Tewkesbury, the Yorkshire Ouse to Selby, and on the Mersey, the Manchester Ship Canal and the Weaver (where they are called flats) up to Anderton.

Tankers and lighters – the term used to describe barges working within the confines of a port – of varying shapes and sizes, either self-propelled or, more often, towed by tugs can be seen on the Thames as far up as Brentford, the Lea to Enfield and, occasionally, the Gloucester & Sharpness ship canal.

Coastal and small continental ships work up the Weaver to Anderton, the Yorkshire Ouse to Howdendyke and Selby, the Trent to Keadby and Gainsborough, the Yare to Norwich, the ship canal to Gloucester, and the estuarial and river ports of the east coast, like Ipswich, Colchester and King's Lynn, or of the west, like Sharpness and Bideford. Small ships and fishing boats use the Caledonian Canal, fishing boats the Crinan also.

Large sea-going ships navigate the Manchester Ship Canal to Manchester.

The little tub-boats of the small canals of Shropshire and the West Country got a new lease of life as the compartment boats of the Aire & Calder. Introduced in 1862 by the company's brilliant engineer W. H. Bartholomew (who also originally put a tug behind six of them to push instead of pull them and so introduced push-towing to Europe), these have had over a century of useful life. Trains of up to 19 of these compartment boats, locally called pans or Tom Puddings, each carrying some 40 tons and towed by a tug, can be seen carrying smokeless fuel from Doncaster to Goole for export. In enlarged form, carrying up to 140 tons, you can see them being pushed in trains of three by a Cawoods–Hargreaves tug to be tipped at Ferrybridge 'C' power station near Castleford. Similar craft, pushed before a British Waterways Board tug, can be seen on the Trent up to Nottingham, the Aire & Calder to Leeds, and the Sheffield & South Yorkshire to Rotherham.

Many developments are encouraging: specialist craft like steam-heated heavy oil tankers or effluent tankers, or the building of such craft as the four new 800-ton grain lighters that have been built for the Thames grain trade, or *Humber Jubilee* with its telescopic

A British Waterways Board tug pushing two lighters passes Ferrybridge near Castleford on the Aire & Calder Navigation

wheelhouse to enable it to clear low bridges.

Canal tolls are not now collected at toll offices, as they used to be. Instead, each captain carries a declaration of cargo and voyage, except for oil and coal. For oil, a Customs out-turn document is the basis for charging; for coal, loadings agreed with the National Coal Board and Central Electricity Generating Board. Craft are reported as they pass certain points, like Castleford on the Aire & Calder, and at the end of the voyage the document carried is handed or sent to a British Waterways office. From there a monthly toll account is sent to each carrier for payment.

Crew are usually paid by a combination of basic pay plus pay per trip, the latter calculated to take account of overtime, as is necessary in an occupation so governed by varying tide times. On a self-propelled craft, crew duties may include some help with loading and unloading.

Pleasure craft can use all Britain's commercial waterways except the Manchester Ship Canal, for which special permission is needed. But obviously, big transport canals are not the place for beginners, any more than a motorway is for a learner driver. More experienced navigators will find they have added interest because of their working traffic. But it is up to you to keep out of the big chap's way and to give him precedence. He's big, he's in a hurry, and he's doing a job.

The British Waterways Board operates its own commercial craft on some waterways; all the compartment boats working to Goole, the pushed lighters, and a number of barges, most of them in Yorkshire. Most working craft, however, are owned and operated by independent carriers, such as John H. Whitaker Tankers Ltd or Ernest V. Waddington in the north, or Thames & General Lighterage or Mercantile Lighterage on the Thames. Carriers are grouped in the National Association of Inland Waterway Carriers, which deals with the Government and other authorities on matters of common concern. Many also meet with others concerned in the business of freight carrying by waterway in the recently-formed National Waterways Transport Association.

The Board owns certain docks, notably those at Sharpness and Gloucester on the Gloucester & Sharpness ship canal, Weston Point on the Weaver, and Ellesmere Port, this last being leased to the Manchester Ship Canal Co.

The Board has a number of large warehousing depots, as at Brentford, Rotherham or Knostrop (Leeds), and also many smaller warehouses. Some of these, being on canals no longer commercially used, now house goods brought by road, but most are essential to the handling of waterborne cargoes. At some of these depots, notably Brentford, Enfield and Leeds, the export barge groupage services already mentioned are operated: that is, consignments for export can be sent to these depots. There they will be grouped into barges according to the ships for which they are intended, and taken to the docks for overside loading.

Thus waterways work for us as well as provide us with the means to enjoy ourselves.

5 Keeping the Canals Open

Maintenance

To maintain a canal properly requires frequent inspection of the banks to see the first signs of weakening or slipping which, if not at once attended to, might lead to a breach: examination, too, of structures like culverts, bridges, locks and tunnels. Maintenance staff therefore inspect the canal on both banks at frequent intervals, looking at it with experienced eyes.

In the days of horse-drawn craft, bank erosion was not the problem it has become as a result of wash from power-driven pleasure or commercial craft. A walk along any canal will now show the towpath eaten away here and there to a jagged edge, and places on the far bank where small slips of earth have taken place. Waves hitting the canal bank, especially if it is relatively soft and pervious, cause a temporary increase in the water pressure in the soil. As the wave crest passes and the trough comes alongside a section of bank, the water pressure is released and water flows out of the bank. This alternation in water pressures is the mechanism that over the years causes slow erosion, until protective action has to be taken. Boats exceeding the speed limit therefore contribute directly to high maintenance costs and to creating those lengths of piled banks on cruising waterways that are so much less attractive than natural ones.

One can still see examples, usually dilapidated, of the old method of dry walling or timbering the banks, often with hard clay backing also, to prevent erosion. These were not usually taken deep enough, so that water got through and washed out the fines in the soil; the same happened when concrete piles were substituted. Interlocking steel sheeting or piles were then used, the piles being driven well down and backed with a wall of clay to prevent erosion from behind.

Major schemes of bank protection may be the result of sub-sidence. Those who only know the waterways of the south do not realise the effect that this has on canals, as on buildings and all other structures. Three main kinds of subsidence affect the waterways. Most commonly it results from coal or other mining beneath the canal. The ground then sinks within limits that are fairly easily predictable. Again, in large areas of Cheshire and Staffordshire it is caused by brine-pumping, that is, pumping water that has been run through the underground salt deposits, and so become brine, and then separating out the salt in it. The washing away of these salt deposits causes the land to sink, not predictably as with coal mining subsidence, but in any part of a wide area which may happen to be affected by what is going on beneath the surface. Lastly, subsidence may be the result of the canal passing through a bed of moss or peat as at Whixall on the Llangollen Canal. As a result of land drainage, this can slowly dry out and contract, so causing the level to fall. Such contraction is of course common in the Fens.

However caused, subsidence of the ground makes it necessary to build up the banks of the canal in order to maintain the water level. This means that a canal, once level with the surrounding land, will now have to run on an embankment. This has to be constructed by tipping earth and mining refuse, and by building a clay puddle wall along the sides of the canal, faced on the water side by piling. As subsidence gets worse, so do the embankments rise. The canal engineer's aim must always be to keep his protection works a couple of feet above what would normally be bank level, so that a sudden movement of the ground will not cause the water to overflow. He must also fill up the bottom of the canal with mine

The built up canal channel runs high above the effects of subsidence on either side. The Leigh branch of the Leeds & Liverpool Canal at Ince-in-Makerfield near Wigan

Dredging: 'a power-operated grab mounted on a pontoon is used.' In this case a winding hole or turning place is being made at Pool Quay lock on a newly-restored section of the Montgomeryshire Canal

refuse or other material as the banks rise, or the increasing water pressure will burst them. As one walks or cruises along canals that have been affected by heavy subsidence, one can see cracked and wavy concrete walls, maintenance boats dumping material for embanking, and sometimes an overbridge being jacked up to maintain the headroom. Now and then a lock becomes twisted or cracked, and has to be rebuilt. Occasionally subsidence enables a lock to be removed. For instance, it has over the years eliminated one lock at Plank Lane, Leigh, and two at Dover on the Leigh branch of the Leeds & Liverpool, and necessitated two new locks at Poolstock near Wigan, to which a level pound now runs from Dutton stop-lock near Preston Brook on the Trent & Mersey.

The bed of the canal has to be kept clear by dredging out the soil that finds its way into it as a result of bank erosion, and also the rubbish thrown in by the public. This dredging can most economically be done from the bank by using a drag-line or other mechanical excavator, but where this is not possible, as under wide bridges, in cuttings, or where buildings intervene, a power-operated grab mounted on a pontoon is used. On rivers, where shoals tend to form on the inside of bends and below locks, you may see bucket or suction dredgers. I'm always glad that I once saw a manually-operated spoon dredger at work – maybe the last of its kind. This consisted of a large perforated metal spoon on the end of an arm which pivoted on an axle fitted in a wooden frame carried on a narrow boat.

Dredgings are usually dumped into a hopper barge and then taken ashore to be placed wherever the navigation authority can arrange a site with waterside owners: some go to lagoons which so can be built up into good land, some to improve farmers' land, some to special dredging tips. When dredging big waterways, you will sometimes see water being added to the mud in the hopper barge, and the resulting solution pumped ashore. There the solids remain, while the water runs back to the river.

Maintenance of structures must be added to that of the channel. Most British canals are upwards of 150 years old, and their tunnels, aqueducts, bridges, locks, culverts and buildings are all suffering, as humans do in time, from the effects of age. Because some are of great historical interest – many are officially scheduled as ancient monuments or listed as buildings of historic or archaeological interest – and most contribute to the attractiveness of the waterway scene, they have from time to time to be inconspicuously repaired or rebuilt. This comes expensive. In the last few years the Board has had to do extensive work on Anderton lift, Pontcysyllte aqueduct, Harecastle tunnel and Laggan locks, to open out Armitage tunnel, and to strengthen hundreds of bridges under the Department of the Environment's Bridgeguard programme.

Rebuilding a portion of the walls of Blisworth tunnel on the Grand Union Canal in 1977

Lock maintenance, too, is not just a matter of lifting out one standardised gate and inserting another. Because rises vary from lock to lock, and widths, never exactly kept even when locks were first built, have varied more since with slight movements of the ground or the lock walls, each gate has to be made to measure by hand at one of the four workshops at Bulbourne, Bradley, Northwich and Stanley Ferry, and then fitted with a craftsman's care.

Away from the canal the boater sees, other work goes on: beneath, when a culvert carrying a stream under it needs rebuilding, off the line when a reservoir bank demands attention or a water feeder channel has to be cleansed.

In the past, each canal company had a maintenance yard, where lock gates were built, ironwork was forged, timber shaped and carpenter's work done. Many such yards still exist — some of course actively used — and they present pleasant groups of functional and residential buildings: for instance, Hartshill on the Coventry Canal, Hillmorton, now a pleasure cruiser base, on the Oxford Canal near Rugby, Ellesmere on the Llangollen Canal, Bulbourne on Tring summit of the Grand Union, or Northwich on the Weaver with its lovely little bell-tower and clock. The bell called the men to work, the clock gave them the time to end.

In the old days towpaths had to be maintained and hedges cut to keep the path in good condition for the towing horses. These jobs now have to be done so that engineers' staffs can get to the banks at any point where maintenance work has to be done and so that, if a boat has broken down, a man can walk along the towpath to get help, and fitters can get to the boat — this applying to pleasure as to commercial traffic. Motor-driven grass and hedge cutters are increasing the speed with which towpath maintenance can be done, and lessening its cost.

Some maintenance work, as when it is necessary to clean out locks, repoint masonry or replace gates, or repair tunnel linings, involves closing the canal for a time to traffic. These stoppages usually take place in the winter on pleasure waterways, and are listed in advance in stoppage notices which are available to those who need them. Others, often unscheduled, are caused by third-party demands which cannot always be delayed eg to take gas mains or sewer pipes under the canal. Just occasionally, too, there

is an emergency stoppage, perhaps the result of a burst, but these are rare.

Lastly, there may be ice. This is a problem when it forms thickly, though it does not usually stop traffic unless it clogs the gates and paddles of the locks. You can still see moored an occasional ice-boat — a short steel-nosed craft with a rail down the centre to which the men clung as they rocked the boat to break the ice, while a string of horses forced it forward. Nowadays, on commercially-used waterways, ice is usually broken with a steel motor barge or tug or, if it is not too thick, boats are left to break their own.

Sometimes brand-new sections of canal have to be built, perhaps because a road scheme requires a diversion. A recent one was at Stoke-on-Trent, on the Trent & Mersey. First, sheet-steel piling was driven to form the waterway walls; then the bed was excavated, lined with clay puddle and mechanically compacted, after which a layer of broken limestone was laid to show those dredging in the future where the puddle began.

Sometimes also a difficult piece of canal restoration requires new methods. At Limpley Stoke on the Kennet & Avon and Llanfoist on the Brecon & Abergavenny, a 6 in layer of reinforced concrete has been laid on polythene sheeting — the purpose of the former being to prevent water loss through the canal bed, and of the latter to stop the concrete losing water during its curing period. A layer of crushed stone, from which side pipes lead off at intervals, has also been laid to drain any water that may seep through the concrete.

Organisation

The British Waterways Board is not the only British navigation authority: there are also the Manchester Ship Canal Co, a number of Regional Water Authorities, and several local authorities and companies.

However, the Board's organisation may be taken as representative of the others because it arises out of the problems to be dealt with.

The canals are operated by lock, weir and bridge-keepers, and maintained by gangs of lengthsmen — specialised craftsmen who are responsible for the day to day inspection and care of structures and banks, and for doing minor bank protection or repair work. They and many lock and bridge keepers are available to keep pound levels equalised and to operate sluices and water control points at any hour of the day or night, so making sure that heavy rain is run off from the canal before it can endanger the banks.

Twenty or more men will be in the charge of a section inspector responsible for some 30–50 miles of waterway, these in turn being grouped under area engineers. These have some qualified staff who can plan the execution of maintenance works, such as piling and lock reconstruction. Under the area engineers are the reservoir attendants, in charge of one or a group of canal reservoirs.

The Board's waterways are grouped into two regions, north with headquarters at Leeds, and south at Gloucester, each with a principal engineer responsible to the Board's chief engineer in London. The Wigan, Castleford, Northwich and Nottingham areas are grouped in the northern region, the Birmingham, Gloucester and London areas in the southern.

The principal engineers, as well as controlling those at area level, have under them at their Leeds and Gloucester headquarters specialists on the water supply and mining sides, the last-named dealing of course with subsidence problems. The Scottish canals have their own organisation, under an engineer based at Glasgow.

A central engineering services organisation based at Rickmansworth includes sections for the design of engineering works, whether major repair works or replacements of existing structures, including mechanical and electrical items; for the maintenance of plant and equipment; the design and building of specialised inland waterway craft; and for investigating new waterway developments.

The services organisation also includes the repair yards, most of which have plant hire units. Here new craft and items of plant are built and old ones maintained. The repair yards in the north are at Goole, Stanley Ferry (below Wakefield on the Aire & Calder), Newark (Trent), and Northwich (Weaver). Those in the south are at Bulls Bridge (Grand Union), with a subsidiary workshop at Bulbourne, Gloucester and Bradley (Birmingham).

At Board headquarters, there is in addition to the chief engineer, also a chief estate officer to deal with property matters, a director of amenity development in charge of the Board's cruising and amenity work, a director of finance, a director of Freight Services, to run the Board's own trading fleets, warehouses and docks, and the Board's secretary and solicitor.

6 Looking at Canals

I hope that by now you have decided that canals are sufficiently interesting to be worth exploring. It may be that you have booked a passage on a hotel-boat, or hired a craft of your own to wander along them. It may be only that you have decided that whenever you are near a canal you will spend an hour or two on the towpath. Or perhaps you will begin by watching the Kennet & Avon from the windows of a Western Region train on the Westbury line, or the Grand Union from the London Midland track to Rugby.

In this chapter I shall try to describe some of the things to look for; you will find many more for yourself.

Construction

The first canals based themselves on existing navigable rivers, which of course ran at the bottom of their valleys. There was the artificial tributary climbing from the river to a town at a higher level, like the Droitwich Canal, rising by eight locks from the Severn to Droitwich; the canal built to by-pass a bad stretch of river, like the Gloucester & Sharpness; and the canal to join one river to another over a watershed. Canals of this third kind, like the Thames & Severn, are usually heavily locked, have a tunnel or deep cutting on the summit, and a reservoir or pumping station to keep the top level supplied with water.

Other canals are cross-country waterways, such as the Grand Union between London and Birmingham, which follows a fairly straight line. Some of the main cross-country canals meet in Birmingham, which is on high ground, and is therefore approached on all sides by flights of locks.

Again, there are the canals which, like navigable rivers of a similar kind, join a port to its hinterland. Such rivers are the Aire & Calder, converging on Goole and Hull, and such canals as those which, now derelict, used to carry iron and coal down the steep hillsides of Wales to Newport, Cardiff and Swansea. Variants of all these you will find for yourself.

The early canals were contour canals, curving round the contours of the hills rather than cutting across the valleys. In those days, when capital was scarce, it was important to build as cheaply as possible, while the extra mileage of a contour canal did not matter when wages were low and speed was unimportant. Indeed, a winding waterway often tapped extra trade. Later, as wages and speed became more important in relation to the costs of construction, canals became straighter, crossing valleys on embankments and running in cuttings or tunnels through the hills. Therefore the way a canal is built is some indication of its age. The Leeds and Liverpool as it curves round the flanks of the hills on its way from Skipton to the summit is a typical contour canal; the old Birmingham & Liverpool Junction (now the Shropshire Union main line) from Nantwich to Autherley is the opposite, having been built by Telford in conscious rivalry with railways. Between 1829 and 1834 the northern part of the Oxford Canal was converted from a contour to a straight canal, and the explorer can easily find the old curves.

On the rebuilt section of the Birmingham Canal main line between Wolverhampton and Birmingham one can see an example of developed canal engineering in Britain just before it was stunted by the coming of railways. The original line, six locks up to the Smethwick summit and six down again, was reduced by 18 ft in 1790 to 3 locks on each side. Then, between 1827 and 1829, Telford eliminated the locks altogether by a cutting that reached 71 ft deep; the sides of the canal were walled to prevent erosion and increase the cross-sectional area, so reducing resistance to the boats; a towpath was provided on each side, and bridges were built so wide that neither the waterway nor the towpath had to be narrowed. It is still possible to see all three levels at once.

An engineer making a river navigable faced different problems. He was given the waterway, and had to decide first how to maintain a constant depth of water — whether by building weirs to raise the water-level or by dredging to deepen the channel — and second, to what extent he would shorten the river by making navigable cuts across its curves. Most rivers do not have many long cuts, but they form a considerable part of the length of the Wey, the Kennet, and the former Itchen navigations, and of the Aire & Calder and the Calder & Hebble in Yorkshire.

Since many of the midland and northern canals were built, they have faced the problem of subsidence (see also p 52) from coal or salt mining near or under the waterway. The surrounding land may have fallen by anything up to 30 ft and made it necessary to build up the canal banks, raise and re-puddle the bed, and construct such things as waste weirs. Stone or brick overbridges that have cracked are often replaced by timber or steel bridges that can be jacked up if the ground falls further. In places where subsidence has occurred the canals have an odd appearance, for they run well above the surrounding land, as on the Leigh branch of the Bridgewater Canal, and some of the bridges are very humpbacked indeed.

Towpaths

Very early river navigations usually had no towpaths. Barges were sailed or shafted where possible; if towing were necessary, it was usually done by gangs of men (it was then called bow-hauling), who plunged through the obstructions along the edge of the river after hauling payments had been made to the landowners. Towing by men on some rivers, for instance the Upper Medway, lasted until the middle of the nineteenth century, and occasionally in East Anglia to the twentieth. Horses were used for towing on the Thames in the days of Elizabeth I, and came into general use in the eighteenth century. They were not used as lavishly as men, and special towing paths had to be built for them, sometimes by the navigation companies, sometimes, as on the Severn, by separate towpath companies. River towpaths are not usually hedged, and have self-closing gates at land boundaries. In parts of the Fens in the old days towing horses were made to jump fixed gates. When the towpaths changed sides, the horses were carried over in a special horse-boat, or on the Suffolk Stour were trained to jump on to the barge itself and off again.

All canals have towpaths, though now and again, where the canal runs alongside a road, the path will end, for towing used to be done from the road itself. Owing to difficulties with neighbouring landlords or because of the lie of the land through which the canal was being cut, it was quite often necessary for the towpath to change sides, and in this event a roving bridge was built to carry the path over the canal. Sometimes a canal crossed a river on the level; in this case a horse-boat was provided or the towpath would itself be carried over the river on a narrow wooden bridge. I remember a fine example of such a bridge where the Derby Canal crossed the Derwent in Derby, and two of the five bridges that carry the Trent & Mersey's towpath over the river Trent at Alrewas are still of wood.

Most tunnels have no towpath. In such cases the boat was legged, shafted or towed through, while the horse was led over the top. These horse paths can still be walked. A few are specially interesting: Husbands Bosworth tunnel on the Leicester Line runs beneath the railway, but the horse path over the disused track on a specially built bridge; that over the Bruce tunnel at Savernake (Kennet & Avon) dives in its own tunnel under the Western Region main line.

As one walks along a towpath, it is always interesting to look for the marks of towropes on bridges, though the depth of the scores is no indication of the age of the bridges, as the stones may have been replaced. At sharp curves in the canal, or where a bridge stands near a curve, one may find vertical wooden rollers or a protective iron strip to guide the rope, as on the Leeds & Liverpool, or cast iron rollers and wheels, as on the Rochdale.

Most canals were marked with milestones at half-mile intervals, because the tolls were charged by distance. They are mostly simple enough, but some carry pleasantly lettered cast-iron plates.

Basins and Buildings

All canal traffic has a beginning and an end. Traffic gets on to the canal either by being landed overside from ships or loaded from wharf or warehouse, or from a factory or source of raw material. Coal, for instance, was often brought to the canalside in the old days by horse tramroads, and once the position of old colleries is established from the map, it is often possible to find the tramroad embankments. More recently, coal may have been tipped at staithes from colliery railway trucks or lorries. Elsewhere one can see chutes for loading limestone or building stone.

At each end, and at towns on the line, there will be basins where boats could lie, and warehouses where they could load and unload, often under cover. Many of these basins, tucked away in the older parts of towns, and surrounded by warehouses built a hundred and fifty years ago, are very picturesque. Among the best small ones is that at Stourport – a charming eighteenth century group of warehouses, workshops, hotel and cottages grouped round the water – and the lovely groups of buildings at Sowerby Bridge and Driffield in Yorkshire. Of the bigger ones, I especially like Gloucester. At smaller villages along the line, there will once have been a village wharf. The bank is cut back to allow a boat to lie out of the channel, and nearby there is probably a small warehouse, or perhaps a storage basement under a lock house. At junctions of two canals there will be rather more: probably a toll house and two or three warehouses, as at Great Haywood, where the Staffs & Worcs joins the Trent & Mersey, or at Braunston, where the Grand Union joins the Oxford – now converted as a pleasure cruising base.

Each large wharf had a wharfinger's house, and perhaps a crane; locks usually a lock house; movable bridges on big canals some-times a home for a bridge-keeper; tunnels a cottage for the tunnel-keeper, and scattered along the banks, the little houses of the lengthsmen or bank rangers who are responsible for maintenance. These houses can be identified quite easily even on derelict canals after a little experience, and they show in miniature the full move-ment of small domestic architecture, from the charming eighteenth-century cottages built about 1770 on the Staffs & Worcs Canal to the almost Victorian of the Shropshire Union main line and the quite Victorian of the Herefordshire & Gloucestershire extension between Ledbury and Hereford. Some are particularly pleasant, such as the round houses on the Thames & Severn or the little classical bridge-houses of the Gloucester & Sharpness. Some also fall into charming groups, most now well cared for and appreciated. A growing interest in industrial archaeology has led to greater appreciation of the urban canal scene. Not long ago, my liking for industrial and commercial canalscapes, like the Rochdale Canal through Manchester or the spectacular passage through Stoke-on-Trent, was considered definitely eccentric; but now the re-planning of urban canalside areas is causing the old buildings to be cared for and new uses for them to be discovered. Moreover, owners of modern industrial

'. . . the full movement of small domestic architecture. . .'. The canal at Llangollen

'. . . with their curved abutments and the clear oval of their central openings they come gently upon the eye.' On the Brecknock & Abergavenny Canal near Goytre

buildings are, for the pleasure of their own workers, beginning to relate their structures to the water beside them.

Each canal company had its headquarters building: Canal House at Oxford, the Ellesmere Canal building at Ellesmere and that by Northgate locks at Chester are typical.

Bridges

All along the canals are eighteenth- or early nineteenth-century bridges that carry roads or the towpath over the waterway or, under the name of accommodation bridges, link fields or parts of a farm that were severed when the canal was built. Most are of brick, some of stone or iron; with their curved abutments and the clear oval of their central openings they come gently upon the eye. Those of iron offer special visual interest. As well as fixed bridges, some canals have wooden accommodation bridges which either swing to one side to allow a boat to pass, or lift upwards.

The waterway usually narrows for a bridge, and the towpath runs under it. The narrowing is called the bridge-hole. Occasionally one will come across an oddity; a bridge without a towing path beneath it, where in the old days the tow-rope would have been cast off and re-fastened, or one with a slit in its centre to take the tow-rope, as on the Stratford-upon-Avon Canal and part of the Staffs & Worcs, or the picturesque lift bridge at Huddersfield.

Sometimes, too, there are interesting more modern bridges, such as the floating, electrically-operated swing bridges over the Weaver, originally introduced because of the problems created with fixed bridges by subsidence caused by salt-mining, or modern motorway bridges, some outstanding in design. For an interesting bridge complex, try the point in Windmill Lane, Hanwell, where the B358 crosses over the Grand Union Canal at the point where the main railway line passes beneath it or that near Spon Lane locks, Smethwick, Birmingham, where one canal crosses another on the Steward aqueduct, whilst a railway crosses the upper canal and a motorway crosses the lot.

Tunnels

I suppose everyone feels a thrill in a tunnel, but on a railway the speed of the train and the lighted compartment take much of it away. In a canal tunnel, however, one moves slowly to the put-put-put of the engine through an underground world only dimly lit by the headlamp, except where an airshaft throws a circle of light upon the water. The dark and irregular bricks of the curving roof glisten in many colours with moisture, and every now and then a drip goes down one's neck or a thin stream from some small spring patters against one's cap. Behind, the world has gone, and ahead that tiny spot of light will take half an hour or so to become a glimpse of sky.

There were mine tunnels before canals, but when the engineers began to build canal tunnels, they had to learn much that was new. In those days gunpowder was used for blasting, and for the rest it was pick-and-shovel work by the light of tallow candles. Tunnelling from each end was too slow by these methods, and therefore shafts were sunk from the top of the hill to the line of the tunnels, which were then extended in both directions from the bottom of the shafts. In this way, more men could be got to work, and it was easier to dispose of the spoil, hauled up the shafts in baskets by a horse-windlass. The resulting heaps mark the line of many canal

tunnels, notably Sapperton, and are characteristic once one knows their origin. When the tunnel was finished, many shafts were covered, but some were left to give ventilation; they usually now have a circular brick top.

The three longest canal tunnels to be built in this country were Standedge (5,456 yd – later lengthened to 5,698 yd), through the Pennines on the Huddersfield Narrow Canal, Strood (3,946 yd), on the Thames & Medway, and Sapperton (3,817 yd), on the Thames & Severn. The first and last are disused, while that on the Thames & Medway was later divided into two in order to provide a passing place for barges, and in that state is now used as a railway tunnel for trains from Gravesend to Strood and Rochester. The longest canal tunnels in full use are Blisworth (3,056 yd), on the route from London to Birmingham, and Harecastle New (2,926 yd) on the Trent & Mersey, though Dudley, slightly longer than Blisworth, is now once again part of a through route from the Birmingham main line via Parkhead locks to the Stourbridge Canal and the Staffs & Worcs. Harecastle is interesting because alongside the tunnel now in use lies the disused smaller bore of Brindley's original one, the first long canal tunnel to be built in this country, only 5 ft 10 in from water level, and 8 ft 10 in wide. At one time both tunnels were used, boats travelling one way through one and back through the other. Most long tunnels had no towpath through them. Strood and Harecastle New are exceptions, while Netherton (opened in 1858) has two towpaths and was lit by gas, then changed to electricity, and is now without either.

When a tunnel had no towpath, boats might be shafted through, that is poled along by pressing on the sides or roof of the tunnel with an iron-tipped shaft while walking along the boat – a tricky job in the dark – or pulled through by chains attached to the sides. The alternative to shafting was legging. Here is a description of legging a boat through Crick tunnel, written in 1815:

> The tunnel is built of sufficient width to admit of two Boats passing, but our Boat did not come near either side, and to get her through the men laid a plank across the fore part of the Boat which reached near to the sides of the Tunnel – upon each end of this plank a man laid himself down upon his back and their feet touching the wall they push'd the Boat forward by crossing their legs at every step; but had either of them made a slip, the other must have been thrown off his Balance and both of them precipitated into the Tunnel – this was a dangerous and laborious employment, but being accustomed to it, they legged us through in 47 minutes a distance of 1518 yards.

Sometimes the work was done by the boat's crews, later including women, but at some major tunnels, like Blisworth, there were professional leggers.

Attempts were made to draw boats through tunnels with an endless rope driven by a water-wheel, but mechanical traction had to wait for tugs and later for self-propelled boats. These now go through under their own power. In one case, Harecastle New tunnel, which has no airshafts, exhauster fans are fitted at the east end to draw air through the tunnel, and so ventilate it.

Aqueducts

As soon as canals began to be built, they had to be carried over streams or rivers. Brindley was faced with this problem on his first canal from Worsley to Manchester, which had to cross the river Irwell. Opened in 1761, it was a marvel in its time, and when it was demolished to make way for the Manchester Ship Canal, it was replaced in 1893 by another, the Barton swing-aqueduct, the only one in the world. This carried the Bridgewater Canal over the Ship Canal; when necessary the water in the 235 ft long central span can be enclosed, and the whole, weighing 1,450 tons, swung clear of the Ship Canal channel.

Many aqueducts afterwards built are beautiful examples of the engineer's art. Greatest of all is that at Pontcysyllte which lifts the Llangollen Canal on nineteen arches high above the valley of the Dee to Ruabon and Llangollen. Stand in the centre on a windy day, and pay tribute to William Jessop and Thomas Telford, to whom we owe it. Instead of a puddled bed enclosed in masonry it has a cast-iron trough. Telford's first, at Longdon-upon-Tern on the Shrewsbury Canal, still stands, but Pontcysyllte is the perfection of his constructive art. This, and its smaller but still impressive brother of ten arches nearby at Chirk with an iron bottom enclosed in masonry, were intended to carry the main line of the canal from Chester by Wrexham to Ellesmere and Shrewsbury. In the end the canal was built on a different route (see my *British Canals* for the story), and they stand on a branch. Other remarkable aqueducts are those across the Lune above Lancaster on the Lancaster Canal, Dundas and Avoncliffe across the Avon on the Kennet & Avon, Marple on the Peak Forest, those over the Almond, Avon and Water of Leith on the Edinburgh & Glasgow Union, the Kelvin on the Forth & Clyde in Glasgow and the Stanley Ferry tied-arch aqueduct near Wakefield.

These are among the greatest, but all over the canals, used and derelict, will be found smaller and usually pleasing specimens of one, two, or three arches which are well worth a scramble into the fields alongside to see. Look for them wherever the Ordnance Survey map shows a sizeable stream crossing the canal. Usually aqueducts carry the canal over a stream, but occasionally over a road, in which case the road may have been lowered for the purpose. Very often the places where the canal engineers altered the routes of roads in order to carry them over or under the waterways can still be traced. Sometimes, again, instead of carrying a stream under a small aqueduct, the engineer led it into a circular stone basin, whence it ran in a syphon pipe downwards and under the canal and so to its old bed.

When the railways came, they brought with them a new kind of aqueduct, for the engineers sometimes had to sink their line below a canal, enclosing the existing waterway in a trough, as at Frimley on the Basingstoke Canal or Halberton on the Grand Western. The same has happened with new roads: the Alperton aqueduct over the North Circular Road is worth visiting.

Stretton aqueduct carries Telford's Shropshire Union Canal main line over Telford's Holyhead road

Water Supplies

A canal lives on water. To retain it, the bottom and sides are puddled; that is, clay worked up with water has been spread over them in layers altogether about 18 in to 2 ft thick, and then consolidated – in the old days this was sometimes done by driving cattle over it. Sometimes the sides only were puddled by making two vertical clay walls, the bed making itself watertight by the deposit of fine material. Occasionally a section of canal runs through ground naturally watertight and needs no puddling; occasionally too, leakage has been so bad that sections have been concreted, as at the eastern end of Sapperton tunnel. Watertight side-walling or piling as a protection against erosion is now common.

Water has also to be supplied. Most canals change level in their course. Some, like the Leeds & Liverpool or the old Huddersfield Narrow, cross an obvious watershed by climbing up one side of a range of hills, tunnelling through the top at the summit level, and descending the other. Many pass one or more much smaller ones, for every summit level is on a watershed. Others climb up a valley to a terminus at the top, like the Cromford, the Peak Forest, or many of the Welsh canals.

Water is needed to replace that lost by leakage, evaporation and seepage, or used by lockage, but the main problem of supply to a canal is that of keeping the summit level full, because on the one hand, being the highest level, it will be above many sources of supply such as springs and streams, and, on the other, it is always being drained by the water used at the locks at each end. One lockful of water is needed to pass a boat on to the summit, and another to pass off it at the far end. A narrow lock of 8 ft depth holds about 28,000 gallons, a broad lock 60,000 gallons or more.

Moreover, most rain that produces effective run-off into reservoirs and canals falls between October and March. But about three-quarters of all pleasure boat movements now occur between May and September, one-third of the year's total being in July and August. Maximum use of water therefore takes place during a time of minimum run-off from rainfall and maximum evaporation loss from heat and seepage loss because land alongside the channel is so dry.

Water supply to summit levels is usually derived from special canal reservoirs, like those near Tring on the Grand Union, themselves supplied, with or without pumping, from streams, wells and drainage. Many of these reservoirs are beautiful artificial lakes, such as those at Earlswood on the Stratford-upon-Avon Canal; nowadays such reservoirs are often used for sailing and recreation. When the canal is disused, the reservoirs are still enjoyed; the old reservoir of the Wilts & Berks Canal at Coate Water near Swindon is a pleasure lake and that of the Bude Canal at Tamar Lake a bird sanctuary.

Additional water is obtained from natural run-off, rivers, and also wells, streams and springs if the Acts of Parliament under which the canals were built allow it. These rights are limited, because when canals were promoted, water in streams and rivers was a valuable commodity. It drove mills for grinding corn and for all kinds of industrial purposes, and therefore canals got their water rights only after much opposition from millowners. Sometimes the proprietors had to deepen the summit level so that water that would last for a week could be run into it on Sundays, when the mills were not working, as on the Stroudwater; sometimes they had to pay the millers for the water; sometimes they had themselves to buy up the mills. Nowadays there are few water mills, but instead we have taken much of the water that once ran in country rivers, and diverted it to urban water supplies. Canals play their part in this supply; for instance, water from the Dee at Llantisilio is now run through the whole length of the Llangollen Canal to Hurleston reservoir, whence it is used for public supply. This arrangement probably ensured that the canal was kept open.

These water supplies from reservoirs or streams are led into the canal by feeders, which are themselves occasionally navigable. The waterway from Trevor to Llangollen is in fact a navigable feeder — hence its narrowness.

Sometimes canal reservoirs have to be built below the summit-level if they are to collect enough water; sometimes also water has to be pumped from wells, as used to happen on the Thames & Severn at Thames Head, or from a lower level of canal back to a higher, as in Birmingham where water is pumped back from the Walsall to the Wolverhampton level to be used again, or from the river Don at Tinsley back up the flight of canal locks to the Sheffield level. In such cases, one can sometimes find interesting old pumping engines, like the Boulton & Watt beam engine at Crofton on the Kennet & Avon, open to the public. Their buildings too should be noted – for instance, that at Leawood near the Derwent aqueduct on the Cromford Canal, or that at the bottom of Braunston's lock flight on the Grand Union. As well as water used for lockage, or lost by leakage, seepage or evaporation, much is sold for industrial use to help pay maintenance costs, though most of this is returned after it has been used. Water control is helped by a network of flow-gauging points on feeders, reservoir readings, pumping station records, and other evidence of water levels and movements.

In summer, water supplies tend to be low. In winter, canals are usually full and are prevented from overflowing by side weirs which carry surplus water into the nearest stream, and by hand-operated sluice gates, which can be worked by the lengthsman. Surplus water also runs in side channels round locks or by weirs from a higher to a lower level until it can be got rid of over weirs or through sluice gates.

On rivers, where there may be a rapid rise in the water level after heavy rain, and where there are no side weirs, the water has to be moved quickly down the stream by opening the weir sluices alongside the locks, these being regulated as necessary to obtain a more or less constant level.

Here and there along a canal you will find the waterway narrowing for a few yards. At the narrow part there may be a single pair of gates set flush into the sides of the canal, or a vertical slot running down the stonework. If the latter, there will be a pile of thick wooden planks nearby, sometimes stored in a wooden or concrete shelter. These are stop-gates or stop-planks. If a burst should occur in the canal bank, the gates can be shut, or the planks dropped into the slot, so isolating the damaged part and preventing more serious flooding of the countryside. Stop gates are usually placed at convenient places along the line of the canal, and in addition on each side of an aqueduct or a big embankment, since these are especially vulnerable to leakage.

Locks

Canals in this country have used three means of overcoming differences in level – locks, inclined planes and lifts – and each has many variations. Unlike a canal, a railway line can be built on a slope, the engine using more power going up than coming down. The same applied to unimproved river navigations with their natural current. We have seen that flash-locks and weirs first enabled rivers to be built up into a staircase. With flash-locks, however, the whole pound (the length between two weirs) above a barge had to be emptied and then refilled to allow it to move a step upwards. It was far more economical of water to concentrate the step in a small place, by means of the pound-lock, what we mean nowadays when we talk of a 'lock'.

The pound-lock consists of a chamber enclosed by two sets of gates, of equal height at the top. The inner edges of the gates are set in vertical heel-posts, which turn in recesses cut in the stonework of the lock, called quoins. The vertical posts at the outer edges of the gates are the mitre-posts or breasts; they come together at an angle pointing towards the upper pound, and are kept shut by the weight of water above till the lock is filled. The bottom gates reach to the level of the bottom of the lower pound of canal, which is also the level of the bottom of the lock itself. The top gates are shorter, and reach only to the bottom of the upper pound of canal, the space below being filled with a stone or brick wall called the sill. Gates are almost always of wood, but a few are made of iron or steel. The bottom gates are fitted with openings covered by movable doors, usually called paddles (cloughs in the North, racks in Ireland), which can be opened to allow water to leave the lock or closed to retain it. The top gates may also have paddles, but set in the wall of the lock on each side of them will be channels into which paddles are set, controlled by paddle-posts beside the lock. These channels admit water to the lock. The method of working a lock has already been described. On the bigger commercial waterways the gates are power-operated.

Most locks are built with a chamber of brick or stone, though at Beeston on the Shropshire Union there is one built on running sand, and made entirely of cast-iron. Some old ones, however, had sloping turf banks and timber framing to stop boats going aground, but this type was wasteful of the water which soaked into the turf banks when the lock was filled. On narrow canals some locks have a single top gate and two bottom gates; elsewhere most have two gates at each end. There are a few locks – for instance on the Nene River and at King's Norton on the Stratford-upon-Avon Canal – which have one or two vertically-rising or guillotine gates. The lift of a lock may be from a few inches to about 14 ft, though the new Kennet & Avon lock at Widcombe, Bath, has a lift of 19 ft 5 in; the average is about 8 ft.

Locks may be found singly, or may be closely grouped in a flight. The two biggest flights in the country are those of thirty locks at Tardebigge on the Worcester & Birmingham, and of twenty-nine at Devizes on the Kennet & Avon. When locks are arranged in flights in this way, the drawing of water from the summit can be reduced by using side-ponds, placed beside the lock. When the lock is emptied, approximately the first half of the water is run not into the lock below, but into the side-pond; next time the lock is used, this water is used to half-fill it. Thus each use of the lock draws only about half a lockful, and not a whole lockful, of water from the summit. A variation of this system is to put two locks side by side, and to use the first half of the water from one to half-fill the other.

A short flight of locks was sometimes built as a single structure without intermediate pounds, the top gate of one lock being the bottom gate of the next. These are called staircases or risers. This system was economical of land, and useful where the hillside to be surmounted rose steeply, but it had two disadvantages, the great height of the gates, and the fact that a normal-sized boat has to move one way through the whole flight before a boat coming the other way can start. Therefore it is extravagant in water and wasteful of time. Pairs of locks built in this way are quite common. At Bingley in Yorkshire, on the Leeds & Liverpool Canal, there are two groups of broad locks, Bingley Five-Rise and Bingley Three, which are most impressive, and at the Northgate, Chester, there is a staircase of three locks remarkable for being partly cut out of rock. On the Caledonian Canal, the eight locks at Banavie are a staircase — here called Neptune's Staircase. The top of a flight or staircase often offers a special excitement, for instance at Foxton on the Leicester Line, or at the top of Bath locks on the Kennet & Avon; one floats high up and sees the canal line dropping excitingly to the valley below.

Several special kinds of lock are to be found on working and derelict canals. When a canal gives on to the sea or a tidal river there is a sea- or tide-lock, usually of the normal kind which allows a boat to lock down from the canal into the tideway. Such tide-locks, however, sometimes have four sets of gates, two facing each way, so that a canal boat can lock either up or down according to the state of the tide.

Where two canals join there is often a stop- or regulating-lock, the purpose of which is to keep the water supplies of the two canals separate. In the old days each company jealously guarded its own water, and often it would agree to join another canal only if it were guaranteed against loss of water. Sometimes this meant that there was no physical connection at all. At one time this was the case at Worcester Bar in Birmingham, where all goods had to be transhipped over a narrow wall from one canal to another. Where a physical connection was made, a stop-lock was usually built, even though, as at Marston, where the Ashby Canal joins the Coventry, there is normally no difference of level. A stop-lock guaranteed that the only water lost was that actually used in passing a boat through the lock; which way it was lost depended upon the relative heights of the two canals at the time.

Locks are always worth looking at: the design, size and type of paddle-gear vary greatly, for each canal company had its own ideas. Here and there on disused waterways one will find older types; for instance, on the Suffolk Stour the lock gates were swung on hooks and rides like field gates, and therefore the heel-posts had to be joined together at the top by galley beams to prevent them falling inwards. The lock chambers themselves had wooden floors. So did many early locks, especially those built in marshy ground. Look also at the brick or stonework of the steps down to the canal, the cobbled or bricked treads of the towpath slope and of the segment of circle built to prevent your feet slipping as you push the lock beams.

Inclined Planes

In some hilly parts of the country the slopes up which canals had to be carried would have demanded flights of locks expensive to build, wasteful of time and extravagant in water. Therefore inclined planes were substituted. These were steeply sloping railways that connected the upper and lower pounds of canal. In some cases goods were transhipped at the top of the plane to trucks which carried them down to be replaced in other boats at the bottom: the plane at Morwellham on the Tavistock Canal was of this kind. In most, however, a small tub-boat, usually about 20 ft long and carrying some five tons, was itself carried up and down the plane, either in a caisson full of water, or dry in a cradle. The caisson or cradle was held level because the back wheels were taller than those at the front. On two canals, the Bude and the Torrington, the boats themselves were fitted with wheels. Most inclines, again, had double lines of track, so that one descending boat was to some extent counterbalanced by another going up. Motive power was either by steam engine, waterwheel, or a bucket-in-a-well system by which a huge descending bucket full of water pulled the boat up the plane.

A number of these inclined planes were constructed during the canal age. The first was on the Ketley Canal in Shropshire. It was built by William Reynolds the ironmaster and completed in 1788. There were six in Shropshire, fifteen at one time or another in Somerset, Devon and Cornwall, three in South Wales, and one underground in the Duke of Bridgewater's mine at Worsley. The

78

'. . . bricked treads of the towpath slope. . .' the ridges there to give horses a grip. Farmer's Bridge locks on the Birmingham Canal Navigations

last is not accessible, but most of the others can be visited* though rails have been taken away and only grassy slopes remain. The plane at Morwellham on the Tavistock Canal had the greatest vertical rise, 237 ft (though it carried trucks, not boats, cargoes having therefore to be transhipped at the top) followed by that at Hobbacott Down on the Bude Canal, 225 ft, and at The Hay, Coalport, Shropshire, 207 ft.

Most of these early planes were out of use by the end of the nineteenth century: the last, at Trench in Shropshire, ceased work in 1921. Before then, however, two much bigger inclined planes had been built as part of the spasmodic process of modernising canals. One, at Blackhill on the Monkland Canal near Glasgow, was built in 1850 to replace a flight of locks. It ceased to be worked about 1887. The other, at Foxton on the Leicester line of the Grand Union, was opened in 1900, again to replace locks, and was not used regularly after 1910.†

There are two large inclined planes on the Continent, at Ronquières (Belgium) taking 1,350 ton barges, and Arzviller (France) for those of 350 tons.

Lifts

By means of inclined planes boats could be hauled up a slope from one level of canal to another. Alternatively they or their cargoes could be lifted vertically. An early example of a canal lift is at Hugh's Bridge on a branch of the Duke of Sutherland's Tub-boat Canal, in Shropshire. Here the branch canal, $43\frac{1}{2}$ ft below that of the main line, entered a tunnel that brought it almost under the upper pound. From the side of the upper pound a shaft was sunk to the tunnel, and coal carried in containers was then lifted from a boat in the upper pound and lowered down the shaft into another boat in the tunnel. This lift was later replaced by an inclined plane.

A number of lifts of different kinds were then built experi-

* See my *The Canals of the West Midlands* for those in Shropshire, *The Canals of South West England* for the West Country planes, and *The Canals of South Wales and the Border* for those in Wales. Morwellham and The Hay have been partially restored under industrial archaeology programmes.

† For Blackhill, see Jean Lindsay, *The Canals of Scotland*; for Foxton, see my *The Canals of the East Midlands*.

mentally, but the only ones to be regularly used on a canal in early times were the set of seven on the Grand Western Canal in Somerset and Devon, between 1838 and 1867. The principle was that two caissons were suspended from wheels mounted on a central axle. Each caisson could hold a tub-boat, and the lift was worked by adding water to the uppermost caisson till it began to fall, when it raised the other. The vertical rise of these Grand Western lifts varied from $12\frac{1}{2}$ ft to 42 ft.*

In 1875 a much bigger canal lift, still working, was opened at Anderton to transfer boats from the river Weaver to the Trent & Mersey Canal, so shortening the distance between the Mersey and the Potteries. It has two caissons in which boats can float, each holding two narrow boats or one barge. At first the caissons counterbalanced each other, one going up as the other came down. The power was hydraulic, partly supplied by adding water to the top caisson and partly by an accumulator. Later the lift was converted to electrical power, and the two caissons are now worked independently. Anderton lift was the prototype for a number of continental lifts in France, Belgium and Germany, and for two in Canada.

Bits and Pieces

All along the canal you will see bits and pieces of history. Stone or iron milestones or boundary markers, iron lock number plates on the balance beams, sometimes bridge nameplates (as on the Staffs & Worcs Canal), old notices.

Towns and Villages

The buildings of towns and villages, the fields and lanes of the countryside, lie round a canal as it takes its curving course across the land. When canals were built, their basins were put as near as possible to the towns they served, but could seldom be carried into an existing built-up area. Each of these basins created its own canal suburb, like the part of Paddington around the basin behind Praed Street, itself named after William Praed, the first chairman of the Grand Junction Canal Company. In any town Canal Road or Wharf Street was the way to the basin.

* See my *The Canals of South West England* for fuller details.

As one walks along the towpath of a canal towards such a basin, one passes between buildings that were built later than the canal and enclosed it in the growing town. The years roll back and one enters an earlier time. The world of the towpath is a world that began about 1760 and on the whole ended about 1850. The warehouses may be of old dark brick, designed with an eye which looked to the appearance as well as the use of a practical building, perhaps with a cupola, as at Stourport, or a graceful curve to the tops of the windows. Some straddle the canal so that goods can be hoisted straight out of the boats into storage, many offer a wooden awning or a covered entry into which the canal boats can slip, like that mysterious specimen above Camden locks on the Regent's Canal.

Factories or mills stand on each side of the canal. They may have changed hands several times since they were built, and take their supplies now by rail or road, but one can usually trace the original wharf that lay between them and the water, or discover the branch canal that once ran into their yard or underneath their building so that goods could be loaded or unloaded vertically.

Rows of brick workmen's cottages face the towpath, built for the boatmen and warehouse workers; there will be the remains of stables dating from the days of horse towing, and a smithy that will now be something else. Somewhere about will be the wharfinger's house, somewhere the toll-keeper's office, somewhere perhaps a mission-hall to boatmen, and somewhere a pub.

There are some towns that were built because of a canal and for a time at any rate owed their existence to it; Ellesmere Port, Runcorn, Stourport, Sharpness and Goole are some of them. Goole for instance, was built by the Aire & Calder, and declared a port in 1828. There are canal villages too, often at junctions, such as Barbridge, where the Middlewich branch joins the Shropshire Union main line. There are the lines of red-brick cottages, the warehouses on each side of the canal, and facing the branch the public-house that recognised that canals run to the sea by calling itself the Jolly Tar Inn. But everywhere the canal runs it will be lined by streets, houses, fields, that conform to its structure, and which took life from it and contributed in turn to it again, and often do so still. Look for instance at the placing of the buildings, the roads, the mills, as one walks down the Thames & Severn and Stroudwater Canals along the Stroud valley from Chalford to the Severn.

Everyone who enjoys waterways has his favourite canal pub, and I shall not tell you mine. But names are worth noting, general like The Navigation, The Canal Tavern or The Wharf; concerned with craft, The Keel or The Paddington Packet Boat, the latter being a passenger boat which used to run between Paddington and Uxbridge where the pub is; with carrying, like The Boat and Horses; with canal structures – The Big Lock, The Aqueduct, or Tunnel House; with canal names – The Calder and Hebble or the Grand Junction Arms; or with personalities, such as The Duke of Bridgewater.

The floating restaurant is a recent development. You can now eat and drink while moored, for instance on the *Barque and Bite* on the Regent's Canal by the Zoo. You can also do so while cruising on the Thames, the Oxford Canal, Regent's, Edinburgh & Glasgow Union (at Ratho), and, by the time these words are in print, probably elsewhere also.

The canals and rivers are there; I suggest you go and explore them.

7 Searching Out the Past

So far I have assumed that the canals you will be exploring are still navigable, or are being restored. There are others. A hundred years ago one could have heard along them also the clippity-clop of the towing horses or the rush of water into a lock, but they were the weaklings, and when competition came they were crowded out and died. Some were formally abandoned by Act of Parliament and some by Board of Trade warrant; some were discarded by railways that had bought them, and others built upon; and some just faded away, when their shareholders, overburdened with debts, no longer came to meetings where someone might suggest yet another passing round of the hat to keep the waterway open. The process began as early as the eighteenth century, when the unfinished St Columb Canal in Cornwall was allowed to decay, and only ended when in 1963 the British Waterways Board decided that the smaller waterways had a future for pleasure cruising as well as a working past.

I confess that such derelict canals have a fascination for me. I am not one of those who would rather have lived a hundred or two hundred years ago, who rail at the worst things of today and compare them with the best of yesterday, and who see the past through the double lenses of make-believe and ignorance of what the past was really like. I have read too many canal records for that. But to admit that the canal age, and still more the age of railway and canal competition, was a harsh and in some ways primitive time for men and horses alike, does not mean that one ignores the very great contribution the canal promoters, engineers, managers, boaters and animals made to the prosperity of the country, and of their own countryside. Their monument lies from Cumbria to Kent, from Inverness to Cornwall, and from Powys to the Wash. So, perhaps, behind the sheer pleasure of exploring, and the added pleasures of recognition of the original purposes of things long disused, there is also something of piety, of a tribute to those who built as well as they could. Their works are crumbling now, but once they were good, and had their day.

All those canal features that I have described in the section on

'Looking at Canals' can be found on those that are derelict, if you don't mind rough going, have a seeing eye, and know where to look. Derelict canals of any size (but not derelict river navigations) have been listed in Ronald Russell's invaluable book, *The Lost Canals of England and Wales*, which outlines each canal's history and what to look for. When you have chosen one, trace its course as well as you can on the 1:50,000 Ordnance Survey map.

Most canals are partly marked, and it is not difficult to fill in the rest of their courses by remembering that they usually follow the contours, except where there are inclines or locks. If, as sometimes, the 1:50,000 maps are uninformative, consult the $2\frac{1}{2}$ in, or the 6 in or 25 in plans in the British Museum or the local reference library, preferably in early editions. For the sites of town basins, warehouses, canalside buildings and wharves, try old town plans in the local Borough Engineer's office, or, if you have not time for that, ask if 'The Wharf' survives as an address, or if there is a Canal Street or Navigation Road in the town. The remains of a wharf can be found in any fair-sized town or village that lay on a canal or navigable river. Such wharves can usually be traced; for instance on the Wye, and on the disused part of the Severn they can be seen at Shrewsbury, Bridgnorth (where the marks of the towing ropes are still on the parapet of the bridge), and round Ironbridge. All up and down old canals one can find buildings called 'Lock House', 'Wharf House', or 'Canal Cottage'.

I hope I can tempt you into exploring derelict canals and navigations. I do it not just because I am interested in them, but because of the odd parts of the country into which they take me, and of the people I meet. One plods across fields, struggles through woods, squelches through mud, in places where no tourist ever goes. The people one meets, naturally courteous to those they think lunatic, are at once interested when one mentions 'the old canal', and soon one has been introduced to grandfather, who remembers it working, or whose cousin was a boatman, or whose wife was the daughter of the last lock-keeper, and so the talk starts, much of it accurate, a little naturally wrongly recollected over the decades.

It is best to explore in winter or spring, before the undergrowth is too thick, especially if you want to take photographs. Your oldest clothes and Wellington boots are recommended. As rich sites of undisturbed nature, derelict canals, like old railway tracks or quarries, are wonderfully rewarding. Ruins of wharf buildings can be safe ground for ferns, mosses and lichens, fresh even in winter. In old lay-bys tall reeds, rushes, mace and sedges rustle their dried stalks in the old whisper, 'King Midas hath asses' ears', that children hiss to each other by the Thames & Severn, and

'As rich sites of undisturbed nature, derelict canals are wonderfully rewarding'. A disused section of the Basingstoke Canal

shelter the little brown reed bunting who pipes hopefully in cold weather. On brick remains of shed or engine house a robin is sure to appear from nowhere and expect a sandwich crumb.

Much of your exploring will be across private lands, and it is right to be punctilious in asking permission, in your own interests as in those of explorers who will come after you. Some towpaths of derelict canals are, however, rights of way, eg those in Leicestershire, and lengths of the Thames & Severn Canal in the Cotswolds.

Let us explore two canals together, and see what there is to find.

The Oxford Canal Curves

Between 1829 and 1834 the upper end of the Oxford Canal between Braunston and Hawkesbury was straightened, and the total length of the canal shortened from 91 to $77\frac{1}{2}$ miles. It is often thought that Telford was the engineer, but this is not so. Sir Marc Brunel and Charles Vignoles made the survey, and William Cubitt had overall responsibility for the work. Most of the curves of James Brindley's original contour canal are visible on the map and traceable on the ground as they cross and re-cross the existing line. The following itinerary for a short visit will take you to the most interesting parts.

If you take the A426 Leicester road out of Rugby, in about half a mile after the beginning of the dual carriageway the road will pass over the main line of the canal just short of Brownsover. At this point a 20 ft broad path of water leads northwards half way up the green valley side. It is a ruminative stretch, full of weed and water-lily, but still deep and able to reflect the tall poplars, guelder roses and bending willows that shade its bank. This is the beginning of the old Cosford loop that ran up one side of the valley and down the other, one of several parts of the old curves still to hold water. It was cut off when the new line was built across its foot.

Go on for a short distance, take the first turn on the left, and stop by a bridge where you can see the old canal curving across a field. Walk across the field and climb up on to the green bank of the towpath, and you are on a raised marshy track with may-bushes growing on it. The field falls away to farm buildings and ducks and sheep panting in the summer heat, but high up on the canal-bed you view them with peaceful detachment. Further on an aqueduct carries your track high over the deep green valley and the shining water of the little river Swift, a tributary of Shakespeare's Avon. In a straight line down the valley from the aqueduct you can see the far-away spire of Rugby parish church. The aqueduct has two wide arches, and when I was there, I heard no sound but swifts overhead and a distant tractor in a field. From here the old canal crossed the road and continued as far as the old railway embankment before turning back to run parallel to the road for a few yard at the Rugby end.

From Cosford go to Newbold-on-Avon, and walk up the yard of the Boat Inn behind the pub to the main line. You come suddenly out on to the towpath. To your left the curve swings into Newbold tunnel. It has two towpaths, and was built during the operation of straightening the curves.

The old line left the new to run past the Boat Inn into a tunnel that carried it under the main road and the churchyard. Its subsidence can be plainly seen across the mown grass of the churchyard entrance, and my companion said he had observed it sinking over the years. Through the beautifully-kept churchyard and past the high red stone tower a path dips steeply down to a stile and a field, and to the right is the old red brick entrance to the tunnel. Beside the mouth are two giant ash trees, as tall as the church tower above, and below the scorings of old towlines can be

seen upon the brick entrance arch. The tunnel is used as a cow shelter, and a low wall has been built inside the entrance. The canal goes on from the tunnel, looking like a gentle slope down to the hedge at the bottom of the field.

Lastly, you can trace the old loop that runs round the village of Brinklow, now full of broad beans, plum trees and potatoes in allotments, and then make your way to the main line as it crosses the Smite brook. On the east side you will find a solid embankment, but if you cross by the footpath alongside the brook, you can see on the other the remains of an older twelve-arched aqueduct. Indeed, you will have passed beneath one of its widened arches. The old aqueduct only had a narrow boat channel so that no passing was possible; during straightening the embankment was added to enable the canal to be widened.

Bude Canal

The Bude was a remarkable canal, the longest of those built for tub-boats. No other reached 350 ft from sea-level within six miles; no other had six inclined planes; and no other, perhaps, leads one to quieter or more beautiful places. It was built to carry shelly sea sand, used as a fertiliser, and coal inland from Bude harbour. It begins at Bude as a barge canal and runs a short way to Helebridge near Marhamchurch, where the tub-boat section begins. Thence it rises by two planes to Red Post, where it divides into two. One

The Bude Canal: 'built to carry shelly sea sand, used as a fertiliser, and coal inland from Bude harbour.' The path sloping down to the right is the formation of the horse tramroad that once brought sand dug on the beach up to the tub-boats waiting at the wharf

branch runs downwards by three planes, at Merrifield, Tamerton and Werrington, to its terminus near Launceston, the other to Blagdonmoor near Holsworthy with one rising plane near Venn Farm, at which point it is joined by the water-feeder from Alfardisworthy reservoir, now called Tamar Lake.

Many days can be spent exploring this canal, and especially the Launceston branch, but I assume here that you have a car and only one day to spare. If you approach the canal on the Bideford–Holsworthy or Hatherleigh roads, begin at Blagdonmoor, $1\frac{1}{2}$ miles north-east of Holsworthy, which was the terminus of the Holsworthy branch. The area of the basin is difficult to determine precisely as it is now weed-covered, but some buildings remain, including a single-storey warehouse, stables and cottages. The canal was to have continued farther, and beyond the buildings an unfinished cutting leading to an intended tunnel can be seen.

Then go on to Venn Farm, north of the Holsworthy–Stratton road, and ask permission to walk along the canal towpath, or look at the canal from the many small bridges that cross it. The feeder and part of the old canal, as I write, still bring water here from the reservoir, to be piped to supply Bude. This section, together with the Tavistock, are the only tub-boat canals in the country of any length still holding water. They are worth seeing because they emphasise how small these canals were, in their time the equivalent of the light railways of the later nineteenth century. Turn left at the waterworks, and you will reach the top of the Venn (Veala or Vealand) inclined plane. Especially in the spring, walk down it and along the primrose-bordered towpath to the single-arched aqueduct over the Tamar, the bases of the arch deep in anemones.

Return to the Stratton road and go on to Red Post. The junction of the two branches lies in a field to the left of the left-hand road. (Go down the road for 100 yd, and turn in at a field gate just past the hump in the road that marks the old canal bridge.) Go back to the Stratton road and on for $1\frac{1}{2}$ miles to a point where the old road forms a lay-by on the left. A gate here is labelled: 'Public footpath, Hobbacott Farm'; from it a track leads to the top of the Hobbacott Down incline, and a broad view over Bude Bay. Envy the job of the incline-keeper as the sun sparkles on the sea and the larks sing overhead, but remember also the winter gales and the rain that

A lane dives under Werrington inclined plane

sweeps in from the Atlantic. This smooth slope of turf running down the hill between hedgerows was the second highest inclined plane on canals in Britain, with a rise of 225 ft. It was originally worked by the power of two huge buckets of water which alternately drew up a boat as they descended in their wells. One of these wells can be found, but the squat stone building has gone which housed the steam-engine used when, as often, something went wrong with the bucket machinery.

The old track from Hobbacott to Marhamchurch plane is mostly rough and overgrown, and at the Marhamchurch end passes through gardens. But you can drive to the foot of Marhamchurch plane by way of Stratton. At the foot of this plane lie the Helebridge wharves, warehouses and workshop, where merchandise was transhipped from the broad canal that runs to Bude. Walk down the towpath to the first lock, then return to Helebridge and drive through Marhamchurch and into the lane that leads by Cann Orchard to the Red Post–Werrington road. From this lane you will get a good view of the Hobbacott Down plane from below.

Merrifield and Tamerton inclined planes can be found by noticing on the map where the canal's track cuts the contour line. Merrifield still has its wheel pit but Tamerton's has collapsed. The third on the Launceston branch, usually called the Werrington incline, is built across the lane that runs down the western side of the Tamar a little above Bridgetown, and forms part of the farmyard of the farm there. The wheel pit for the waterwheel that provided power to pull boats up can be seen, with the farmer's permission, beneath the top end of the plane. A little farther on, at Crossgate (Druxton) is the grassed-over basin with its wharfinger's house, warehouse and stable, that ended the Launceston branch.

One of the tub-boats, fitted with wheels underneath to run on the inclined planes, can be seen at Exeter Maritime Museum. For a full history and itinerary of the Bude Canal, see *The Bude Canal*, by Helen Harris and Monica Ellis.

If you want to go further into the history of derelict waterways than Ronald Russell's *The Lost Canals of England and Wales* takes you, consult the various volumes of the 'Canals of the British Isles' series. The following suggestions for exploration are grouped by the volumes of this series, which are also the divisions of Ronald Russell's book. Where the canal has its own published history, I have starred it.

South West
The Chard, Grand Western* (part), Torrington, Bude*, Liskeard & Looe* and St Columb Canals: the Parrett Navigation.

South and South East
The Somersetshire Coal*, Dorset & Somerset*, Wilts & Berks*, Stroudwater, Thames & Severn*, Salisbury & Southampton*, Portsmouth & Arundel*, Wey & Arun Junction*, Royal Military* and Thames & Medway Canals: the Itchen, Arun, Western Rother*, Sussex Ouse and Medway (unfinished part above Tonbridge) Navigations.

South Wales and the Border
Monmouthshire (2 lines), Glamorganshire, Swansea, Neath, Tennant, Kidwelly & Llanelly, Herefordshire & Gloucestershire and Leominster Canals: Wye Navigation.

West Midlands
Shropshire, Shrewsbury, Duke of Sutherland's Tub-boat, Montgomeryshire, Shropshire Union (Weston & Quina Brook branches) Canals.

East Midlands
Charnwood Forest branch (Leicester Navigation), Oakham*, Grantham, Nottingham, Nutbrook*, Cromford, Trent & Mersey (Uttoxeter branch, Froghall to Uttoxeter), Chesterfield (upper part) Canals: Melton Mowbray (Wreak) Navigation.

North West
Manchester, Bolton & Bury, Rochdale, Huddersfield, St Helens, Carlisle Canals.

Yorkshire and the North East

Dearne & Dove, Barnsley, Market Weighton, Leven Canals: Driffield, Foss, Swale, Bedale Beck and Codbeck Navigations.

Eastern

Horncastle, Caistor, Louth, Wisbech, North Walsham & Dilham Canals: Sleaford, Welland, Bure, Ipswich & Stowmarket, Blyth, Stour Navigations.

Scotland

Edinburgh & Glasgow Union, Forth & Clyde, Aberdeenshire Canals.

When you've explored all the British disused waterways, you can then go abroad to start afresh, in the United States, where many enthusiasts do it, in France, Ireland and elsewhere.

8 Meeting Others and Doing Things

I hope that by now you feel that canals offer many kinds of interest. In this section I have collected some other aspects: one or other of them may appeal to you.

Canal Restoration

The idea of restoring a former transport route with volunteer labour stiffened by professional advice and help, and perhaps then running the reopened line largely with amateurs, goes back to 1950. In that year L. T. C. Rolt, author of *Narrow Boat* and first secretary of the Inland Waterways Association, turning back to an earlier love, founded the Talyllyn Railway Preservation Society to acquire and restore a derelict Welsh narrow-gauge quarry railway. In that year too, the Lower Avon Navigation Trust was incorporated with C. D. Barwell as chairman, the Lower Avon Navigation, 28¼ miles from the Severn at Tewkesbury to Evesham, having been bought early that year by Barwell and the Inland Waterways Association. Both succeeded. The railway opened in June 1951 and still flourishes; the Lower Avon, presenting a more formidable task of reconstruction, was reopened to Evesham in 1962, after £35,000 had been raised apart from tolls by the Trust's near-1,000 membership.

Restoration of the Lower Avon was followed by the lower part of the Stratford-upon-Avon Canal. This famous 13 miles was restored from 1961 onwards by the initiatives of the Stratford-upon-Avon Canal Society, the Inland Waterways Association and the National Trust, the energy of David Hutchings, the work of soldiers, prisoners and volunteers, and money raised about equally from public and private sources. It was reopened in 1964. Later, David Hutchings and the Upper Avon Navigation Trust began work on the difficult restoration of the old Upper Avon navigation, disused for nearly a century, between Evesham and Stratford, and completed it in 1974.

At the end of 1962 the British Waterways Board succeeded the

British Transport Commission. The Board and the Staffordshire & Worcestershire Canal Society started talks on the restoration of the 16 locks at Wordsley on the Stourbridge Canal, and the reopening of the route that way between the Staffs & Worcs Canal and Birmingham. They agreed to share the work and the cost, volunteers rallied and enthusiasts subscribed, canal staff enjoyed a new and rewarding relationship, and in 1967 the Stourbridge line was reopened. Before then, however, similar talks had been held with other societies, notably the Kennet & Avon Canal Trust on the restoration of that lovely waterway between Reading and Bath, and the Caldon Canal Committee (now Trust) on what could be done to reopen the canal between Stoke-on-Trent and Froghall, a most beautiful stretch of waterway.

The pattern was emerging – collaboration between the Board and a local society, itself supported by enthusiasts generally. When restored, the waterway to be maintained and managed by the Board. However, a source of funds additional to those of the Board and the societies was lacking until s.114 of the 1968 Transport Act authorised local authorities to provide money for amenity and recreational waterways, and s.109 the transfer of amenity waterways to local authority care. Under the second power the Grand Western Canal in Devon has passed to the Devon County Council; under the first the restoration idea has spread quicker than any of us in those days dared to hope. The Ashton and Lower Peak Forest Canals between Manchester and Marple, the Caldon and Erewash have been restored. Long stretches of the 75-mile long Kennet & Avon between the Thames at Reading and Bath are already navigable, along with parts of the Pocklington, Yorkshire Derwent, Basingstoke and others. Still more, like the Montgomeryshire, Grantham, Wey & Arun, Rochdale, Stroudwater and Thames & Severn, queue up for attention.

Recently, the government's job creation scheme has made unexpectedly large sums available for canal restoration, on condition that the work is used to train young craftsmen. Under it, for instance, the difficult de-watered section of the Kennet & Avon at Limpley Stoke is being tackled, several miles of the Rochdale Canal are being restored, and even such unlikely candidates as the

Neath and Tennant Canals in south Wales have not been forgotten.

Here, then, in canal restoration is work to be done and fun in doing it. General responsibility for any piece of restoration lies with the British Waterways Board for canals under their control,

'. . . in canal restoration is work to be done and fun in doing it.' Volunteers at work upon the Basingstoke Canal at Fleet

like the Montgomeryshire. Their engineers plan the work to be done in consultation with the local canal society, and a decision is made upon what is best carried out by Board staff, and what by volunteers. With non-BWB waterways, various arrangements exist. On the Rochdale, a Rochdale Canal Trust is being set up as controlling authority.

Locally, volunteer work is organised by the appropriate canal society – the Kennet & Avon Canal Trust and the rest – but assisted greatly by Graham Palmer's merry men (and women) of the Waterway Recovery Group. If you subscribe to the magazine *Navvies* (currently 50p or more post free from Graham Palmer, 4 Wentworth Court, Wentworth Avenue, Finchley, London N3 1YD), the magazine of the Group, you will learn what work is going on, on what weekends, where, and what help is needed. You will be surprised at how much is being done. You will also be welcomed by a local canal society if you have a special favourite, and want to concentrate on its interests.

Canal Societies

There are dozens of these (see Appendix 2) and at least one among them should offer you interest and enjoyment. Nationally, there is the Inland Waterways Association with its many local branches: an organisation for pressing the canal case, amenity and commercial alike, upon the authorities, but one also which through rallies, meetings, its magazine *Waterways* and so on, offers everyone a means for finding out what he or she would specially like to do. It is paralleled by other Inland Waterways Associations for Scotland and Ireland.

Scattered through the country are local canal societies: some regional, like the East Anglian Waterways Association, most concerned with a single waterway or group. Some, like the Pocklington Canal Amenity Society, were founded with restoration especially in mind; others are concerned to watch over active waterways, to give a hand with their care, encourage the authorities to maintain them well, promote their active use, and study their history. Societies like the Staffs & Worcs Canal Society are like this. Others again, like the Wey & Arun Canal Trust, care for the remains of a derelict waterway, and have hopes of future restoration.

The pattern of societies' life varies, of course: in the summer, rallies, club cruises, and restoration or maintenance working parties; in the winter, lectures, quiz programmes, slide and film shows. All have bulletins or newsletters, and all bring together a mixed bunch of people who enjoy canals.

Parallel to the canal societies are the boat clubs – groups of people, mostly but not entirely boat owners on some stretch of water or in one area, usually with club premises. In the summer the clubs run rallies, cruises and competitions; in the winter dances, parties and similar social events: the emphasis is more on boats, cruising and social life, and less on the maintenance or restoration of the waterway. Some are suited by one or the other: some by both. Information about boat clubs from the Association of Waterways Cruising Clubs, Sec: J. C. Cotterill, 34 Allman Road, Birmingham B24 9DR.

Rallies

Most love rallies; some quite like them; a few don't like them at all. But they are very popular, not only with canal enthusiasts, but with the locals of the place where they are held, for by their means many get their first introduction to canals. Rallies may be run by the Inland Waterways Association – they put on one national and several branch rallies each year – canal societies and boat clubs. Those of boat clubs are usually for their own members, but IWA and society gatherings are open to anyone.

Most rallies are held over a weekend. Boats from far and near gather at the chosen spot, moorings being allocated by a berthing steward. Once there, you can take part in on-the-spot competitions, watch such events as the narrow-boat tug-of-war, explore the trade and other bankside tents, join in the various sideshows and events, and get to know other enthusiasts. Usually also there are rally awards. For instance, at IWA national rallies, there is one for the most enterprising voyage in getting to the rally by a first-time rally attender. You needn't, of course, arrive only by boat – just go. There will be much to interest you in the bankside tents and events, and in strolling along the towpath to look at the boats.

If you haven't a boat, a rally is still great fun, and a good introduction to the world of the canals, and the people who inhabit it.

Young People

Many youth clubs, like Beauchamp Lodge at Little Venice or that with the pirate's castle on the Regent's Canal, have found that canalling offers young people many kinds of interest. Local education authorities or public libraries can give local information about the kind of activity.

History and Museums

John Burns once called the Thames liquid history and created a lasting phrase. All waterways are liquid history, some of which goes back two hundred years or more. It can be approached in two main ways: by reading what has been written, and then maybe oneself tackling old records or newspapers to enlarge what one has found out; or by what is now called industrial archaeology – that is, studying remains on site, and so complementing what the records reveal.

For this, the relevant body is the Railway & Canal Historical Society, with a membership of some 500, several local branches, a *Bulletin* and *Journal*, and programmes of winter lectures and meetings and summer visits which cover both kinds of study. For those interested in waterway history as a part of transport history generally, there is the Transport History Group. Many local canal societies also take an interest in history – some, like the Dudley Canal Trust, a great interest. So also do many county or regional local history and industrial archaeological bodies, and many town and village historical societies also.

You will find some canal histories listed in Appendix 1. Most will be found on the Inland Waterways Association's sale shelves, at canal shops, or at the bookshop run by the publishers of this book, Baker Street Bookshop, 33 Baker Street, London W1M 1AE.

The Waterways Museum (Stoke Bruerne, near Towcester, Northants NN12 7SE: tel Northampton 862229) quite near the M1, is run by the British Waterways Board. Write, enclosing a sae for a leaflet on opening times – it is open almost every day of the year except winter Mondays. The Museum has a fine collection of canalia, housed in an old three-storey canalside building in one of Britain's prettiest canal villages. The South Yorkshire Industrial Museum (Cusworth Hall, Doncaster DN5 7TU: tel Doncaster 61842) has a canal room containing a mainly Yorkshire collection. The North Western Museum of Inland Navigation at Ellesmere Port in Cheshire maintains a collection of waterway craft. Enquiries to Dr David Owen, The Museum, Manchester University, Manchester M13 9PL.

For other museums with waterways collections, see Appendix 3.

Catherine of Aragon approaches the Waterways Museum at Stoke Bruerne

Lectures and Courses

Most canal societies and local branches of the Inland Waterways Association and the Railway & Canal Historical Society arrange winter talks for their members on all aspects of waterways.

In addition, adult education colleges and similar bodies organise weekend and longer courses from time to time. Particulars are usually given in the Inland Waterways Association's *Waterways* or the Railway & Canal Historical Society's *Bulletin*. Any and all help to provide a background to one's interest in the waterways.

Civic Schemes

A few years ago, not many local authorities saw possibilities in their local canals: most barely tolerated the dirty and rather decayed stretch of urban waterway that passed through their

Beneath one's feet brick treads; above one's head an iron footbridge; beyond, the 'Long Boat'

town; a few wanted it drained and filled in. Things have changed since then. Officials and councillors have realised that canals are often the only open water a city has, towpaths the only footpaths. And so a movement has grown up to turn urban canals into amenities, a pleasure to residents and an attraction to visiting cruisers. This may mean a facelift for the buildings, including repair, repainting and judicious additions, or it may mean new buildings, the scheme however incorporating what can be used of the old. Some nostalgic enthusiasts prefer picturesque decay to modern landscaping and urban architecture, but most like such revivified scenes as surround the 'Long Boat' by Farmer's Bridge locks, Birmingham (a few minutes from New Street station). This idiom is of the 1970s and not the 1870s, but today canals are living and not, thank Heaven, stuffed or a kind of linear folk museum. The movement includes opening urban towpaths for walking – for instance, along the Regent's Canal and the old Grand Junction in London.

All over Britain town canalscapes are altering. Even when a canal is irretrievably gone, its former track can still serve people well, as Swindon shows in the use to which it has put the Wilts & Berks' old track through the town. Here is a specialised interest for those many concerned people who work as officials or councillors of local authorities, or in the ranks of amenity societies.

Fishing

Canal fishing is popular, as can be seen any weekend on almost any waterway. Fishing rights may lie with the owner of the bank or with the British Waterways Board, and in either case may be let to a fishing club. Local enquiries will usually tell you the situation: otherwise consult the *Waterway Users' Companion* (BWB), or ask the nearest British Waterways Board office or officer. Kenneth Seaman's *Canal Fishing* is a useful book.

The Naturalist

Our ancestors looked at canals, as we do, but were more familiar with nature. They expected fine elm and beech trees to frame a bridge or mark a turn, thick clumps of dogwood, wayfaring tree, maple or blackthorn to keep off wind, strong flowering may hedges to protect crops from towpath men, and well-stocked farm fields or mine sites to provide traffic on the canal in fertiliser or coal.

In spite of all changes and building, canals can give us basically the same natural beauties. In fact, others have developed, as water-loving trees and plants have grown and fish have increased. Frogs, voles, snakes have followed, and then heron and kingfisher and their kind, and even otters in turn have followed to feed on them. Ducks, swans, moorhen, coot, are all naturalised on canals, and our wealth of native and migrant birds feed among the reeds and shelter in towpath hedges and copses in the fields along the way. Warehouses and industrial buildings backing on to the quiet waterway are much used by birds and even by bats, when empty; decaying buildings are their delight. On derelict canals, half-sunken boat timbers can be brilliant with dragonflies. This marvellous world is seldom found by road and rail users, but is ready and waiting for anyone in a cruiser or canoe, or walking the towpath. The password is 'quiet and easy'.

As soon as spring begins, the water's edge is scattered with gold kingcups, and catkins on alder, hazel or poplar show their russet or yellow. Snakeshead fritillaries are returning to cherished Thameside meads. Along the Wey, Lea, Thames, the open stretches of the Kennet & Avon, the leafy Stratford or pastoral Oxford and its curves, blackthorn, wild plum or cherry blossom catches the light in brilliant patches, making you reach for your camera. Woods give off the smell of wild garlic, as the derelict Thames & Severn does for lilies of the valley. Green-purple lances of reeds start up through last summer's dry brown, and the embroidery of pondweed and delicate water plants and sturdy water-lily leaves spreads along the canal line.

Birds and beasts are busy with nests and young ones — ramshackle moorhen and coot nests along the edge, ducks', reed bunting and warblers' well hidden in reeds. On a sunny April day by Marple aqueduct on the Peak Forest I saw a frog with a little frog on her back swim across the canal, both clear yellow and green speckled. Dusk brings out the hedgehogs, and along the Kennet & Avon's towpath by Dundas aqueduct I once met a mole padding steadily on a sponsored walk.

Swan parents teach their chicks to navigate the Oxford Canal

With summer the water plants bloom in hundreds and the young creatures get active. Families of downy ducklings, coot and moorhen chicks have to be edged out of the boat's way, and rarer sights can be seen. A pair of kingfishers with a young one beside them on a low branch beside the Wey was a pleasant sight, or terns from the sea fishing the quiet waters of the Lea. A heron will rise up suddenly as you come round a bend and flap off, legs trailing, in front of you to the next bend, settle down till you arrive, and take off again. You can travel along with him, sometimes with a pair, till he at last decides to break back or you, overcome by guilt, decide to stop for lunch and give him a rest. With luck you might see the line of a snake, only the 'S' curve of head and bit of neck above water, crossing the canal, or hunting frog, fish or tadpole.

On the outskirts of Midland towns the late afternoon can bring the little owl from old factories to hunt young mice and insects along the canal. When you moor up at the end of the day and the engine falls silent, you will hear rustlings and plops in the water as voles or rats seek their supper, and fish jump at insects low over the surface. Even rabbits get bold enough to be watched as they nibble juicy plant and grass tops, while the air is full of birds' twitterings after the silence of the afternoon. Buntings, warblers and tits seem less shy at this time of day, especially if the boat is still and the engine silent. Equally so, in the early morning some birds and small animals seem almost not to be aware of the boat and will give you a close, almost a friendly, look.

September and October seem special to northern waterways, which tend to leave the low land and climb round the shoulders of hills. You can look down on farming valleys turning yellow and gold with late harvest, or on close-confined towns marking the structure of the hills, and then up at hilltops thick in colour-changing trees or with jutting rocks glittering here and there with minerals. Silence seems deeper here than in fertile valleys, the world farther away. Sunny days bring out more butterflies, and when your engine stops at lunch time you can hear the crickets, and maybe see one, clipped to a stiff stalk. The summer's growth of weed (many interesting kinds, not just the Canadian!) and rushes, and such handsome plants as water parsnip, Himalayan balsam or purple loosestrife decorate and colour each stretch of water. Small birds are gorging on seeds and insects among the reeds, and this is a chance to see a goldfinch or a bullfinch.

The important thing with the world of nature is to look, and look closely. If you let it drift past you like pictures in a town museum, it will offer you nothing, and you will never know the pleasures and the marvels you have missed. But once you have got into the way of looking, a book on water birds, water plants, small animals, insects or wayside trees and shrubs, will help you to see more, so that you will come back from your cruise or walk richer then you went.

9 Going Abroad

British waterways are so interesting that it is easy to be content with them. Yet, across the Channels, on the Continent or in Ireland, are other waterways, very different of course, and yet in some ways surprisingly familiar. The same is true of north America.

In this chapter, then, you will find comments on overseas waterways, the sections being arranged in the same order as those of this book.

Canals for Holidays

There are three ways of holidaying on an overseas waterway: on a passenger-carrying craft, a hire cruiser or a boat of your own.

Passenger-carrying craft

These may be the sort of craft on which, like a miniature cruise liner, you can book a cabin and then sit comfortably in a deck-chair watching the scenery and the traffic. I myself find waterway cruising so much more interesting than on the sea, for one is never out of sight of land, and always one has the choice of three sights – each bank, and the every-varying scene of the waterway itself.

The best-known cruising ground is the Rhine — steamers take 4/5 days for the Rotterdam–Basle run, and there are several lines, offering different degrees of comfort, to choose from. Some boats take in the Moselle to Trier as part of a Rhine cruise. The upper Rhine locks, the Rhine gorge and Lorelei rock, and the Moselle winding past castles, vineyards and such delightful little towns as Cochem, Traben–Trarbach and Bernkastel, are especially worth seeing.

The Danube is an unusual, interesting and somewhat awesome river. Passenger craft work between Passau on the German–Austrian frontier and the Black Sea, though shorter trips are available. They offer a simple way of seeing behind the Iron Curtain, and of visiting the two pairs of great new locks, and the hydro-electric works, at the Iron Gates gorge that pierces the Carpathians between Yugoslavia and Rumania.

Smaller craft run from Stockholm to Gothenburg via the Göta Canal. Because our own Thomas Telford was employed as consultant, its locks curiously resemble those on the Caledonian Canal. Other passenger boats run on the Weser in Germany, the Seine. Yonne, Marne, Rhône and through the Burgundian canals in France, and through Holland — these last especially popular in tulip time. Similar services operate in the United States, eg along the Mississippi, the Atlantic Intracoastal, or the New York State Barge Canal, successor to the old Erie.

Trip Boats

All over the Continent and North America you can also find trip boats, based on river and canal towns, and offering day trips. By working out a motoring route that takes you to canal towns, you can explore a lot of waterways in this way, or, by hiring a car abroad, you can plan a holiday partly on a passenger craft, and partly using trip boats. For information on services, seek advice from each country's tourist office.

Hiring, or using one's own boat

Pleasure cruising, whether with hired cruisers or one's own boat, is not common on Continental waterways, but is increasing. All Continental waterways — well over 10,000 miles of them — are open to the cruiser, most free or at very low charges. Some are quiet and peaceful, carrying little commercial traffic, like the Canal du Nivernais in France; most carrying barges in quantities from few to very many, and of varying sizes (there's no need to be frightened of these, once you know the drill). A few of the biggest, like the Rhône and parts of the Rhine, are not for amateurs unless accompanied by a pilot. For the beginner, France, Belgium and Holland are the best countries.

Cruising the Shannon

Canals at Work

Inland water transport has developed very differently in Britain and on the Continent. There the great rivers and their tributaries, and later canals built from them, were from mediaeval times the main means of internal transport and of international trade. Roads were their feeders, and only where no waterways ran was road transport much developed. Continental governments therefore planned and financed major new waterways as contributions to economic growth, recognising the basic truth that good transport and plenty of power underlines all such growth and is precedent to it. When Louis XIV helped to finance Europe's first major watershed canal, the Languedoc (now the Midi) from the Mediterranean to the Garonne leading to the Atlantic, 240 km long with 101 locks, the reason was economic development. Opened in 1681, eighty years before our own Bridgewater Canal, it is still there for you to visit. It showed what could be done, and so Governments and local authorities continued the waterway-building policy. When railways came, they were considered to be complementary to the waterways in which so much public money had been invested. This attitude has persisted. Therefore continental countries are accustomed to think of waterways, railways and roads as forming a single transport system in a way we have never done.

In western Europe, therefore, waterways are important carriers of goods, inside each country and across national boundaries, for a barge loaded in France may unload in East Germany or Poland. Small barges of less than 100 tons capacity are seldom seen: the smallest commonly in use are the 250–350 tons craft of the average French waterway. In France most canals have been built, or rebuilt, to the minimum Freycinet standard lock of 38·5 m by 5·2 m enforced by a law of 1879, and the barges have conformed. Bigger barges can be seen on the larger rivers and canals of the Continent: most are about 500–700 tons, but on bigger waterways still, equivalent to motorways, the standard is 1,350 tons, and on the Rhine and similar rivers one sees 1,500, 2,000 tonners and more. Most are self-propelled, or push-towed in pairs, one behind locked to another in front and pushing it. Occasionally you will see a tug with a string of barges behind her. On larger waterways push-tugs have in front of them two, four or more lighters, all worked as a single unit. Among them you may see LASH or Seabee lighters from the barge-carrying ships.

Like railway waggons, barges can be built for special purposes – tankers for wine or oil, container carriers, chemical barges, motor-car transporters, and so on. You'll find an interest in spotting these.

In north America little remains useful of an extensive canal system that was energetically built between 1800 and about 1850, with the aim, firstly, of joining New York and the Hudson river to Lake Erie by means of the Erie Canal, and then other east coast ports to rivers (notably the Ohio) behind the Allegheny mountains by other canals. Secondly, of linking the Ohio itself to Lake Erie and so in turn to the Erie Canal and the east. In its place has grown up, mainly since 1900, an enormous water transport system mainly based on the Mississippi, its many tributaries, and a canal link with Chicago and Lake Michigan; and on the two Intracoastals, the Gulf and the Atlantic, which between them provide a sheltered waterway from near the Mexican border nearly to New York, interrupted only by the peninsula of Florida. In Canada, however, the early locks and by-pass canals that made the St Lawrence navigable from the sea to Lake Ontario, and the early Welland Canal opened thence to Lake Erie, have been repeatedly enlarged into the present St Lawrence Seaway, a joint Canadian–United States enterprise.

Apart from the seagoing ships and Lakes freighters of the Seaway, the usual commercial craft of north America is the Jumbo lighter, 195 ft by 35 ft carrying 1,500 tons, a group of these being pushed by a large push-tug. LASH and Seabee lighters (two Seabee lighters = one Jumbo) are also often included in the push-tows.

Looking at Canals

Everything described in Chapter 6 can of course be found on continental canals – all that, in many different forms, and varied scenery too.

Read up the areas you are going to visit well before you start: do some careful planning; and take a colour camera or a cine-camera with you. Over the years you will bring back a storehouse of memories, pictures on the mind and screen.

A downbound towboat pushing 14,100 tons of coal enters McAlpine locks at Louisville on the Ohio River

Locks

For instance, the many varieties of lock. Even those that broadly resemble our own mitre-gated pattern have endless varieties of detail. And one can find magnificent lock staircases – Béziers on the Canal du Midi in southern France is famous, but try Scandinavia and see those on the Göta Canal in Sweden, and on the Halden and Telemark Canals in Norway.

Bigger locks may have vertically-rising gates that slide up through a superstructure towering above the lock entrance, under which craft pass in and out. Others have falling gates, disappearing beneath the water, as on the Moselle; or sliding gates, moving sideways to open the lock, as on the Meuse at Nijmegen.

For size, contemplate the staircase pairs at the Iron Gates, each pair with a lift of over 30 m; or the monsters of the Rhône, or, striking not only for their own size but for where one finds them, the huge locks the Portuguese are building on the Douro, that at Carrapatelo having a rise of 35 m, the highest in Europe. The United States has several locks with a rise of over 100 ft, but the world's biggest is claimed by Russia, at Ust-Kamenogorsk in Siberia, with a rise of 42 m. And for sheer interest, visit the series of new and very large locks, complete with multiple side-ponds to conserve water, now being built in Germany on the Rhine–Main–Danube Canal, which has already reached to Nuremberg from Bamberg on the Main, in its climb towards the watershed with the Danube.

Inclined Planes and Water Slopes

Britain has no inclined planes now working. So visit Ronquières, on the Brussels–Charleroi Canal in Belgium about 20 miles south of Brussels, climb the viewing tower, and look at the mile-long incline. Its two tanks or caissons can each raise a 1,350 ton barge (or four 300-tonners) 67 m in 20 minutes. Each tank with its water can weigh up to 5,700 tons, and is carried on 236 wheels running on rails.

At Ronquières the barges are carried lengthwise down the plane, but at Saint Louis–Arzviller on the Canal de la Marne au Rhin near Phalsbourg, not far from Strasbourg in France, they travel sideways. Smaller – this plane takes 350-ton barges – and much steeper, its tanks lift their burdens 44·5 m to by-pass a flight of locks. Each weighs 900 tons, and runs on 32 wheels.

The water slope, opened in 1974, is something new. At Montech near Montauban on the Canal Latéral à la Garonne, the continuation towards Bordeaux of the Midi Canal, the French have built a new kind of alternative to a lock flight. The 3 per cent slope is a concrete flume 443 m long and 6 m wide, giving a total rise of 13·3 m. A diesel-electric locomotive, guided by horizontal wheels pressing against a concrete rail, runs on each side of the flume, the two being linked by a shield. After a barge has reached the bottom of the slope, the shield falls behind it, and is lashed to the barge's stern. The locomotives, moving at 4·5 km/h then push the barge and the wedge of water 125 m long in which it floats, up the flume. As water pressure equalises at the top, the gate holding back the upper canal pound falls back flat to allow the barge to pass out.

Lifts

Britain invented the canal lift, first during the Industrial Revolution, again when James Green built seven of them on the Grand Western Canal in Somerset in the 1830s, and once more at Anderton on the Weaver, opened in 1875. The engineering firm of Clark, Standfield & Clark, who built it, was then commissioned to construct a bigger one at Les Fontinettes on the Neuffossé Canal near Saint-Omer in north-eastern France. With a lift of 13·2 m, it replaced a staircase of five locks, but has itself now been replaced by one huge lock, though the old structure is still there to be admired. The same firm then built four more, bigger and still working, on the Canal du Centre near Mons in Belgium, with lifts varying from 15·4 m to 16·93 m. They are all within some 6 km of one another, at La Louvière, Houdeng-Aimeries, Bracquegnies and Thieu. These all used the hydraulic ram principle.

Germany has built four. Of the two accessible ones (the others are behind the Iron Curtain) one is at Henrichenburg near Dortmund on the Dortmund-Ems Canal. Opened in 1962, it has a lift of 15·85 m and works on the float principle, the caisson riding upwards as floats beneath it rise when water is introduced into the underground chambers where they rest. A newer lift still, counterbalanced this time, is at Lüneburg in north Germany on the new

A tug and barge are pushed up the water slope at Montech

Elbe Lateral Canal. With a lift of 38 m, greater than any so far built, it was opened in 1976.

Should you cross the Atlantic, you can find two other lifts in Canada, at Kirkfield and Peterborough on the Trent Canal between Lake Ontario and Georgian Bay, Lake Huron. These are used only by pleasure craft.

Tunnels

France is tunnel country: she has most of the canal tunnels on the Continent, and the longest still in use. The world's largest and longest, Rove outside Marseilles, 7,120 m long, is closed and may not be reopened, but Bony on the Canal de St Quentin (5,670 m), Mauvages on the Canal de la Marne au Rhin (4,877 m), Balesmes on the Canal de la Marne à la Saône (4,820 m) and Pouilly on the Canal de Bourgogne (3,350 m) are all longer than our own Blisworth. Apart from Rove, there are eight French tunnels over 1,000 m long. Some of the longest, like Pouilly, are worked by a tunnel tug, powered from overhead electric wires, which tows all craft through; craft pass others under their own power. Outside France and Britain, canal tunnels are rare indeed.

Aqueducts

After seeing Dundas, the Lune, Marple, Chirk, Pontcysyllte and some of those in Scotland, go aqueduct-hunting abroad: you will be richly rewarded. Most are in masonry, though on the Dalslands Canal in Sweden I came across the only iron trough I have seen abroad. Outstanding continental aqueducts are the 8-arched one at Minden that carries the Mittelland Canal over the Weser, that at Briare over the Loire, that at Béziers, and that carrying the Canal Latéral à la Garonne over that river at Agen.

Looking for the Past

The United States now has an extensive river and intracoastal waterway system, but very few true canals, and those large. But she has a wonderful collection of derelict waterways, many of which were abandoned just within living memory and well within the age of photography. These have bred a race of canal

The recently-built *Monticello II* cruises a restored section of the Ohio & Erie Canal near Coshocton, Ohio

'buffs' or enthusiasts, who explore their remains, collect the history and folklore of their living days, preserve individual buildings, and press for sections of the old waterways to be included in national parks. Some restoration has indeed been done, notably of the Chesapeake & Ohio Canal, but also of parts of other lines, and several horse-drawn trip-boats are run.

117

Two cruisers are settled on to the cradle that will carry them up the marine railway at Big Chute on the Trent Canal in Canada

Next best is to experience them in the many well-illustrated books and articles that are now appearing, or in the pages of American Canal Society bulletins. To keep in touch, join the American Canal Society; particulars from the secretary, William H. Shank, 809 Rathton Road, York, Pa 17403, U.S.A. For Canada, read Robert Legget's *The Canals of Canada* (David & Charles).

The pleasures of hunting derelict canals can also be experienced both in north and south Ireland. Here you want either W. McCutcheon's *The Canals of the North of Ireland* or V. T. H. & R. Delany's *The Canals of the South of Ireland* as your guides.

So too on the Continent. You will need Roger Calvert's *The Inland Waterways of Europe*, good maps and some knowledge of the language. Try the Loire area in France, or do what I did not long ago, trace part of the old Ludwigs Canal in Bavaria that from 1846 to the end of the last war joined the Main and the Danube, before much of it is obliterated by the new Rhine–Main–Danube Canal.

General

I have listed a few of the great continental waterway sights. They are the highlights: their background is what anyone can see who, with a boat or a car, goes exploring. The poplar-lined waters, the lock-houses, the 'Van Gogh' lifting bridges, the fishermen-thronged canal banks of France: the craft moving against the Dutch skyline; the waterways of Bruges by night; the vine-covered slopes of the Moselle; the endless, hurrying exciting traffic of the Rhine, the long line of the Mittelland Canal stretching towards the east or the graceful towers of the Lüneburg vertical lift etched against the clouds; the pine-wooded waterways of Scandinavia, log rafts bunched against blue skies and white foam boiling out from locks; the low forested banks of the Danube and Budapest's twin cities linked by the Chain Bridge; or the smooth, deep rock walls that enclose Greece's Corinth Canal. Or you may prefer the milder pleasures of the waterways of Eire, with few great sights but many intimacies.

In north America the scale is different: the Mississippi is to the Rhine what the Rhine is to the Severn, and the New York State Barge Canal, a regeneration of the old Erie, is as big as the Continent's biggest. The Gulf and Atlantic Intracoastals are of their own kind – mainly protected sea or lagoon channels, with short sections of true canal. But in Canada you can come nearer to British proportions, with the charming Rideau Canal from Ottawa to Lake Ontario at Kingston, or the long rambling river-lake-canal line of the Trent Canal.

See some of these, and your mind will indeed be rich in beauty and variety of experience, and your slide-cases full of pictures to recall past delights and promise others for next year.

Appendix 1 Finding Out

Short cuts to finding out more about inland waterways are:

(a) Get a copy of the annual *Waterway Users' Companion* from the British Waterways Board, Amenity Services Division, Melbury House, Melbury Terrace, London NW1 6JX. A phone call to 01-262-6711 will tell you the current postfree price.

(b) Buy the monthly *Waterways World*. It publishes a sales list.

(c) Visit the enquiry counter of the British Waterways Board by the entrance to Melbury House, London (it is linked directly to Marylebone station), where booklets, maps and souvenirs are on sale, and your questions can be answered. There you can also see, and arrange to subscribe to, the excellent house journal of the British Waterways Board, *Waterways News.*

(d) Visit the sales office of the Inland Waterways Association on the ground floor of 114 Regent's Park Road, London NW1 8UQ. Alternatively, write (a stamped label would be appreciated) for a copy of their sales List, which includes books, booklets, maps and a range of souvenirs.

You may find the following short list of books and booklets useful:

Background

Inland Waterways Guide, published annually by the Inland Waterways Association.

The Canals Book, The Thames Book, The Broads Book. Each published annually by Link House.

Holiday Cruising on Inland Waterways, by Charles Hadfield & Michael Streat. For those who would like to hire, buy or convert a boat.

Waterways Sights to See, by Charles Hadfield. A guide mainly for the motorist, who may like to look first before taking to the water.

Maps

Two general ones are Stanford's *Inland Cruising Map of England* and Imray's *Inland Waterways of England and Wales*. For specialised maps, see the *Waterways World* and IWA sales lists.

Navigation Guides

Nicholson's four *Guides to the Waterways* (NE, NW, SE, SW) and their *Guide to the Thames from Source to Sea* are invaluable. For specialised guides, see the sales lists.

General Books

I recommend Burton's *Back Door Britain* (an account of a canal cruise round Britain), Burton and Pratt's *Canals in Colour* for the superb pictures, McKnight's *Shell Book of Inland Waterways* for its gazetteer and mass of useful information, and *Waterside Pubs* because one sometimes wants a rest from acquiring information.

History

In pictures, try Ware's *Canalside Camera, 1845–1930*. In one volume form, Charles Hadfield's *British Canals: an illustrated history*, available in hardback and paperback. As a cheap series, the histories of working boats published by Robert Wilson. For history on the ground, Russell's *The Lost Canals of England and Wales*.

The IWA and *Waterways World* sales lists carry many other general and specialised titles.

Overseas

Roger Pilkington's *Waterways in Europe* is most useful. Three books in David & Charles's Holiday Cruising series are Ransom's *Holiday Cruising in Ireland*, Morgan-Grenville's *Holiday Cruising in France*, and Oliver's *Holiday Cruising in the Netherlands*. For readability and amusement, try Morgan-Grenville's *Barging into France*.

For American publications, write for a list to the American Canal & Transportation Center, Box 310, Shepherdstown, W. Va 25443, USA.

Appendix 2 Waterway Societies

There are hundreds of societies, clubs and organisations concerned with one aspect or another of inland waterways. Most of them are listed, with addresses, in the annual *Waterway Users' Companion*, published by Amenity Services Division of the British Waterways Board.

I have listed those with general objects, and a couple outside Great Britain. Of the many others, some are concerned with the restoration, maintenance and development of the waterways themselves; others with some aspect eg cruising, rowing, water skiing. Some are based on schools, universities or other bodies; others are youth clubs. Between them all you should be able to find one or more to suit you.

General

Association of Pleasure Craft Operators – the trade body
Association of Waterway Cruising Clubs
Inland Waterways Association – for all those interested in waterways, from whatever point of view
National Waterways Transport Association – the trade body
Railway & Canal Historical Society
Scottish Inland Waterways Association

Outside Great Britain

American Canal Society, c/o Box 310, Shepherdstown, West Virginia 25443, USA (There are also many local canal societies.)
Inland Waterways Association of Ireland, c/o Terence Mallagh, 2 Clonskeagh Road, Dublin 6, Republic of Ireland (There are also local canal societies in Northern Ireland and the Republic.)

Appendix 3 Waterway Museums

The Waterways Museum, Stoke Bruerne, nr Towcester, NN12 7SE (Northampton 862229)

Bass Museum, Horninglow Street, Burton-on-Trent, Staffordshire

The Canal Exhibition Centre, The Wharf, Llangollen, Powys (Llangollen 860702)

The Canal Museum, The Canal Basin, Mill Street East, Savile Town, Dewsbury, West Yorkshire (Dewsbury 467976)

Cheddleton Flint Mill Museum, Cheddleton, nr Leek, Staffordshire

Dolphin Sailing Barge Museum Trust, Dolphin Yard, Crown Quay Lane, Sittingbourne, Kent

Exeter Maritime Museum, The Quay, Exeter, Devon (Exeter 58075)

Friends of the Black Country Museum Trust Ltd, Tipton Road, Dudley, West Midlands, DY1 4SQ (021-557-9643)

Inland Navigation Museum, 1 St Ives Road, Weston-super-Mare, Somerset

Ironbridge Gorge Museum Trust, Church Hill, Ironbridge, Telford, Salop, TF8 7RE (Ironbridge 3522)

Lancaster Canal Museum and Information Centre, T'owd Tithe Barn, Garstang, Lancashire

North West Museum of Inland Navigation Ltd, c/o Manchester Museums, The University, Manchester, M13 9PL (061-273-3333)

Tiverton Museum, St Andrews Street, Tiverton, Devon

Great Glen Museum, Fort Augustus, Inverness, Highland

Linlithgow Canal Museum, Manse Road Basin, Linlithgow, West Lothian

(This list is taken from the *Waterway User's Companion*, by kind permission of the British Waterways Board)

Index

David & Charles have a book on it

The Shell Book of Inland Waterways by Hugh McKnight.
This comprehensive guide has been compiled by one of Britain's leading experts on inland waterways; it is fully illustrated by numerous photographs and line drawings together with maps of the whole system, ranging from Southern England to Scotland, Wales and the whole of Ireland. Illustrated.

Holiday Cruising on Inland Waterways by Charles Hadfield and Michael Streat includes Stanford's large folding colour map of Britain's canals. With some 3,000 miles of waterway to explore, a map and a locker full of stores, who would not wish to be captain of his boat, for a week, for a fortnight – or for a lifetime?
Here is a readable, practical book by two experts, on inland waterway cruising, and on buying, hiring or converting the boats to do it in. They tell the would-be explorer all he needs to know before he, too, catches the boating bug – virus nauticus, an infection of the head and heart leading to years of happiness. Illustrated.

Holiday Cruising on the Thames by E. and P. W. Ball is a companion volume to *Holiday Cruising on Inland Waterways*. The loveliest of rivers, the Thames, is immensely popular with boat owners and hirers, and very many books have been written about it. Yet for the family taking out a boat for the first – or the twentieth – time, this is probably the most useful. Here is everything inexperienced hirers of motor cruisers want to know, and much that will help the already knowledgeable.
This is more than a book about boats – it is also about the ageless Thames itself. Locks, lock-keepers and bridges; connecting canals, tributary rivers and hidden backwaters; the work of the Authority; boat clubs and the Thames Society; glimpses of history; all unite to produce a book to be used again and again while planning and cruising. Illustrated. *Holiday Cruising Series.*

Holiday Cruising in the Netherlands by John Oliver. Holland is a country of water: of great commercial canals and rivers, of lesser waterways winding past old towns and quiet windmills, of the great Ijsselmeer and little lakes. Well provided with maps and illustrations, this splendid book is packed with necessary information for the man with a cruiser or a yacht. With it, he can confidently explore a lovely country at leisure. Illustrated. *Holiday Cruising series.*

Waterways Sights to See by Charles Hadfield is a friendly inviting book for the family that explores by car rather than by boat. Sixty sights to visit, scattered throughout Britain, are described with affection by the author. All aspects of canals and navigable rivers are here – here a town or village, there a bankside pub, an eighteenth century bridge, a flight of locks, a museum, an inclined plane, a medieval bridge, a Norman warehouse. Illustrated.

Water Byways by David E. Owen. English countryside at its best is as beautiful as any in the world and is most enjoyed at a leisurely pace away from the main roads and great centres of population; many years ago Dr Owen found that the gentle passage of a boat on the canals and rivers was ideal. In this book, his boat *Rose of Sharon* navigates from these into the less cruised waterways and tells of the delights that are still scarcely known. Illustrated.

Waterside Pubs by Ronald Russell. Waterside pubs have never attracted the attention lavished on the coaching inns of the great highways, yet they have their own distinctive charm and interest. Ronald Russell takes a look at their history, architecture and relationship to the waterways by which they were built. Illustrated.

A Canal and Waterways Armchair Book by John Gagg. Canal history holds a wealth of interest in tangible form, from the reasons behind the shape of bollards and bridges to the need for tidal locks or the working of worm gear. In this book, presented for armchair relaxation and browsing, and a companion to his earlier *The Canallers' Bedside Book*, John Gagg has compiled more facts, fun, information and amusement in 100 or so essays on the variety that makes up canal life, history, equipment, and operation.